EVOLVE OR DIE

Lessons for World-Class Innovation & Creativity

TOM TRIUMPH

Ex Innovo Press

Evolve or Die

Thomas Triumph

Typesetting and Cover Design: Kerry Ellis

ISBN: 978-1-7326866-0-1

Dedicated to

Therese, Alexandra, and Tommy

Praise for *Evolve or Die*

"*Evolve or Die* is at once inspiring, entertaining, and thought-provoking. Tom Triumph combines key business insights with his unique narrative style. The result is a must-read for every business executive."

— Kartik Hosanagar, Professor of Operations, Information and Decisions, The Wharton School of the University of Pennsylvania

"Tom shares some simple, actionable advice for all of us on cultivating our superpowers. Read through a series of readable (and sometimes hilarious) stories to change your approach to personal and professional growth, innovation, and the future of work."

— Dave Blakely, Partner, Mach49

"*Evolve or Die* is filled with valuable lessons from successful leaders. With its focus on innovation and creativity, this book will help those who wish to adapt in this ever-changing world."

— Dorie Clark, Adjunct Professor, Duke University Fuqua School of Business, *Entrepreneurial You, Reinventing You, and Stand Out*

"Tom Triumph has artfully captured many of the key lessons in the creative process as he shares real-world stories and experiences across the breadth of science, business, and art and provides simple models to make this all actionable. In a world of increasing complexity, this book is a perfect reminder for anyone looking to push their own limits and explore their untapped potential."

— Andy Walshe, Performance Manager, Red Bull Stratos, program designer for the US Olympic ski and snowboard teams

"Wisdoms abound. Triumph's "simple truths" are entertainingly rich with insights that will help us perform at our innovative best in this complex world. And his generous approach to life is a lesson for us all."

— Carl Nordgren, Entrepreneur, Adjunct Professor, Duke University, *Becoming a Creative Genius {Again}*

"The energy in *Evolve or Die* is the energy of someone who's lived life fully and has not lost that glimmer of 'what is possible' in individuals. Tom takes that energy and gives readers tools and insights in the manner of sitting down over a cup of joe and going over 'the important stuff.' The stuff that matters. Why? Because as you'll discover, YOU matter, more than you possibly know. And this book will help you dial in on that special thing that's you."

— David Brier, Chief Gravity Defyer, DBD International, *Brand Intervention*

"Tom's insightful, enthusiastic, positive, and practical outlook on life is reflected in this book, along with his indefatigable message to keep moving forward to become better each day."

— Livingston L. Holder, Jr., cofounder of Holder Aerospace, former USAF astronaut

Contents

Foreword

As I write this foreword, today is the day that Apple became the first, one-trillion-dollar, market-value company. The Apple I think about most begins with my first impression as I drove up Bandley Drive in Cupertino, California, and saw a pirate flag atop a small, one-story building that could have been any warehouse for any business. It was November 1982 and Steve Jobs had invited me to see his then very secret, insanely great, project he called Macintosh.

I am an insatiably curious person, and I have spent my life wondering why things are the way they are, and why there can't be a better way. As we grow older, we don't get smarter, but we can get wiser. Wisdom comes from learning a context or framework in which to understand your own experiences, particularly one's failings even more than one's successes. I learned that innovation and creativity aren't reserved just for geniuses like Steve Jobs, Bill Gates, and Jeff Bezos. This is a journey that many of us can aspire to and achieve success.

Tom Triumph and I have been friends for many years. He is successful at things that I have never done. Tom is an ultrarunner, and he has the discipline to train daily to be able to run a 50-mile, sometimes even a 100-mile, event. Entrepreneurs by nature are driven people. The good news is, there are lessons one can learn about how to turn dreams into possibilities, and possibilities into probabilities. That's what this book, *Evolve or Die*, is all about.

When most people think of Apple, they think of its great products. I think of the many experiences and resulting stories of amazing people and our trials and errors in the early days of Silicon Valley. Creativity can be learned through a combination of stories, hands-on experience, and hard work. What I love about this book are the many stories and how Tom Triumph has organized these stories into a context that gives the reader a pathway to wisdom.

Many books end up on a bookshelf. *Evolve or Die* should be very near where you work. After reading it, I keep going back to it. I love to randomly open it up to any page and read a few pages, often several times a week. It's a fun experience and very stimulating for anyone with a big curiosity.

John Sculley

August 2, 2018

Introduction

This book is intended for you. Even if we haven't met, it was written with you in mind.

The book contains a culmination of experiences, thoughts, and learning—much of it from world-class innovators and creators. Every single story is true. And every story has relevance to you.

Some common themes will emerge from these stories. Hard work, persistence, courage. Luck is sometimes present. Often, things were learned the hard way. And, as is the case whenever there are innovators and creators involved, there's also a fair amount of love running rampant through the stories. Evidently, *rampant* is how love likes to run—especially when it's heading toward a goal and vision. Perhaps *most* important, you'll see that every one of these luminaries are made—not born.

Here's where you come in.

You've got a lot in common with these folks. Regardless of your current situation, there are stories about regular people in more dire situations and who've attained loftier positions. There are many stories of good, and a few stories of bad. And there's a lot to discover. This book can help you avoid some of the stumbling blocks and help guide you on your journey.

There's something to be learned from—

- someone who ate dog food to survive before creating a multibillion-dollar American media and entertainment company that's known to all of us.

- the globally recognized authority on how people get great at something.

- the woman who's responsible for your first two exams.

- what James Bond has in common with Halle Berry, Sylvester Stallone, and Ed Sheeran.

- the women who created a material five times stronger than steel.

- the key secret of illusionists Penn and Teller.

You'll learn how a frozen fish inspired an innovation revolution, how to overcome a phobia of snakes, and how a world-renowned artist punched fear in the face to strap a paintbrush to his wrist and create works of art. And there are dozens of other stories. This isn't a textbook. It's a collection of real-world stories of innovators and creators, and it's all relevant to you. You can read it by jumping in anywhere and skipping around where it interests you.

Here are a couple of simple truths.

The world is changing rapidly due in part to the ever-increasing advances in technology. Your ability to adapt and learn is more important than ever. The title says it all: *Evolve or Die*. It's somewhat blunt, and it is an exaggeration. But my belief is that it's closer to the truth than many people realize. And it's my genuine hope that this book and the stories within on innovating and creating are of real interest and benefit to you.

It might seem trite to write this, but (in reference to Henry David Thoreau) you weren't meant to settle for a life of quiet desperation. That's said with confidence because—nobody is meant for a life of desperation. You'll need to innovate and create. It's better to learn from the champions, practice like your life depended on it (to an extent it does), and come out strong and punching above your weight (because you can).

You've got a lot to offer this world. We all do. I'm in your corner, offering guidance and cheering for you. Get in the ring, come out swinging, and fight the good fight.

I invite you to visit www.tomtriumph.com and download the free, 52-page, color manifesto titled *The Call to Innovate: Myths, Best Practices and Achieving Your Rightful Place.*

PART ONE

Personal Development

The Roadmap of You

This Is Your Secret Superpower

I have something important to tell you. It's serious, and you should really be sitting down.

Gosh, where to begin. It's big news. So big, you'll have a hard time believing it's true.

Remember when you were young, and you would occasionally wonder if you had some kind of superpower? Kind of like a Ninja Turtle or like Batman or Wonder Woman. You used to wonder if you could accomplish some really incredible things.

Well … You have a secret superpower.

I know this came out of the blue, and you probably don't even believe me. It's a hard thing to even comprehend. You've watched superhero movies, even read some superhero comic books. But, you eventually grew to think superpowers weren't real.

But some superpowers are real. And you have one! The crazy thing is that your superpower has actually been in plain sight your entire life, just waiting to be discovered. Waiting for you to realize its transformative capabilities.

Yet, day after day, you stumbled past its discovery. Hey, don't feel bad. Most people never discover it. But because you didn't learn you had a secret superpower, you blended into the world and lived like most everyone else. Doing the best you could as a mere mortal.

It was the same with me. I didn't know about it either … at least not until this weekend.

This weekend, I found it. I'm not entirely sure how I made the discovery. But once I caught a glimpse, the discovery came quickly. It was kind of like in the movies. Like catching a glimpse of a small, orange glow between the floorboards of the barn, and then finding a spaceship from Krypton hidden below. Kind of like that, but there was no barn and no spaceship.

Once I discovered the superpower, it explained a lot. It shifted my thinking. It was powerful. It explained my past experiences. Why some people do great things. And why often I didn't.

The first thing I wanted to do was start using it. The second thing I wanted to do was tell you.

Before you put on your cape, let me tell you about your superpower. First, the good news.

1. Easy to Use
   Maybe the craziest thing of all … is that using your superpower is really easy. There's basically zero training involved. Think of those Cirque du Soleil performers who juggle flaming torches while riding a bicycle on a tightrope. Learning how to use your superpower is nothing like that.

2. No Pain
   Remember when the radioactive spider bit Peter Parker, and he became deathly ill for a few days before he transformed into Spider-Man? Acquiring your superpower is more like a butterfly landing on your shoulder.

3. No Major Transformation
   Eliminate that image of a person turning into a werewolf, with all that painful body morphing accompanied by bone crackling. Your superpower requires no massive change. Not even a little howling.

4. No Costume Required
   This is one of my favorite features of this superpower … nobody knows you have it. This is a real benefit, because you're not tied to a specific costume, so you can dress however you like. Plus nobody can actually see your transformation, so you don't need to find a place to change costumes. That's convenient, as there are so few phone booths nowadays.

5. No Special Instruction or Teacher Required
   You'd think they'd teach this superpower in school, but I can tell you … no teacher *ever* told me about this. The good news is that no teacher is required.

6. No Permission
   You don't need no stinkin' authorization to use the superpower.
   The superpower fits perfectly in the era described by author and
   entrepreneur James Altucher as "Choose Yourself!" Marketer and
   business thought leader Seth Godin (who also has this superpower)
   would tell you to use your superpower to "Make a Ruckus."

7. You Don't Need an Assistant
   Batman and Robin. The Green Hornet and Kato. You. You don't need a
   sidekick for your superpower.

8. Not Complicated
   No tricky potions to mix. No magic words of wizardry to remember.

9. Minimal Time Required
   It's actually hard to imagine, but this superpower will not take any
   additional time from your life.

10. No Cost
    Free. Free. Free.

OK, it's time you learned of your superpower. Are you still sitting down?

It's the power of 1 percent. By making just 1 percent change at a time,
you can change yourself, your life, and your world. Profoundly.

Let me explain. Better yet. Let me demonstrate the superpower. Please
stand back.

Let's say you start with just one of something. Could be one pull-up, or one
dollar, or one idea. Now, apply your power of increasing that just 1 percent.

It goes without saying, that a 1 percent increase is small. So small, that
you could not even discern a bowl of 100 blueberries versus a bowl of 101
blueberries (superheroes love blueberries).

But if you apply your micro improvement of 1 percent each day for a
year … that 1 will have increased to 37.8 in just a year.

Your superpower of 1 percent holds the key that can lead you to the
greatness you were destined to lead. It's a superpower you share with some
of the most accomplished people in history. People who've attained mastery
in endeavors ranging from music, art, science, athletics, business, and social
work.

Is there a downside? Yes, as with all great powers, the superpower is difficult to acquire. And even for many people who discover the secret, they often fail to utilize the power. Furthermore, it is easily misused. Here's why.

1. Easy to Use
   Because it's so easy to do, it's also so easy not to do.

2. No Pain
   Because your superpower doesn't involve a lot of pain, you might not notice that it's working. Maybe you won't even notice the butterfly landing on your shoulder.

3. No Major Transformation
   Some people want to be heard.

4. No Costume Required
   Some people want to be seen.

5. No Special Instruction or Teacher Required
   Some people want to be told what to do.

6. No Permission Required
   Sometimes we're conditioned to wait for a "go-ahead."

7. You Don't Need an Assistant
   "What?" you say. "You mean I gotta go alone?"

8. Not Complicated
   When it comes to superpowers, the simple often gets overlooked.

9. Minimal Time Required
   How can it be a superpower and not take decades to acquire?

10. No Cost
    Runs counter to the advice of "You get what you pay for."

Let me explain. Better yet. Let me demonstrate the misuse of the superpower. No need to stand back this time.

Let's say you start with just one of something. Could be one pull-up, or one dollar, or one idea. Now, don't apply your power, but rather let it decrease just 1 percent.

It goes without saying that a 1 percent decrease is small. It's 99 nickels lying around instead of 100 nickels lying around (superheroes love Thomas Jefferson, and he's on the nickel).

And if you allow things to micro decrease 1 percent each day for a year … that 1 will have decreased to 0.03 in just a year.

Just as your superpower of plus 1 percent holds the key that can lead you to the greatness you were destined to lead, if your superpower is applied negatively at minus 1 percent, it will lead to mediocrity and disappointment.

And *that* is your superpower that will let you transform just about anything you want. I'm glad you finally know the truth.

Good luck in whatever you choose to do in life. In whatever arena you choose to use your superpower.

I leave you with the words of Commissioner James Gordon from *Batman*. "You're going to make a difference. A lot of times it won't be huge, it won't be visible even. But it will matter just the same."[1]

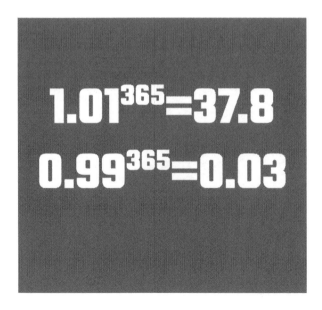

The Most Important Lesson (Never Taught in School)

Of all the things I never learned in school, here's something that should go right at the top. That's saying something, as it seems like there's a million things I didn't learn in school.

It's pointless to blame the teachers for not teaching this lesson.

The nuns in elementary school were preoccupied with the basics of reading, writing, and arithmetic. And the occasional whack with a ruler. The middle school teachers had to deal with our awkward adolescence. High school teachers were focused on their lesson plans. College (and graduate school) brought even greater focus on the coursework material.

For the life of me, I don't know why a single teacher didn't invest just one hour and explain it to me. It could have changed the trajectory of my life and career.

Maybe none of my teachers knew this lesson. But, for whatever reason, this *most important lesson was never taught.*

In the end, I figured it out myself. That's actually not a bad way to learn something. The downside is that it took me decades to figure it out; through working, reading, and living. And painfully—from the real-world experiences of mediocrity and failure. I hate to say those words—mediocrity and failure. But urgh, it's true.

It took a while to figure it out, despite the many clues from life and work along the way. To mention just a few …

Years ago, I heard someone explain that if you sign your signature 10,000 times, the last signature will look almost exactly like your first signature—unless you consciously work to make it different. My signature looks today exactly like it did decades ago.

Once I was training for a marathon where I wanted to do well. So, I'd significantly increased my weekly mileage and sustained that high-training mileage for months. Throughout this period, if the training was a 3-mile run or a 20-mile run, I habitually ran at the same pace—which was p l o d d i n g. The result? My marathon time was slower than prior times trained on a fraction of the mileage. Basically, I'd spent hours training to run slowly.

On the workfront, I've experienced various endeavors that never improved much beyond the performance metrics I'd achieved early in the project. My team hit average milestones week after week, month after month. Maybe you can relate.

So what's the most important lesson (never taught in school)?

It's a fundamental lesson that specifically explains how to improve. And it works for a great many things. It's been studied for decades, and it's probably been known by many people for centuries. Yet, it was something nobody ever explained to me.

It's called purposeful practice, and it's actually easy to understand.

The best person to learn it from is Dr. Anders Ericsson. Dr. Ericsson is a globally recognized authority on improving human performance. He's a professor of psychology, has conducted many illuminating studies, written countless peer-reviewed professional papers, and authored several books. Basically, Anders Ericsson knows how people get great at something.

It turns out, there's no magic involved with purposeful practice. And the good news ... there's *lots* of good news.

Purposeful practice is all of the following.

- Proven (it's practically a law of the universe)

- Simple to understand

- Consistently shown to be the factor in moving good to great

- Applicable across disciplines, including music, sports, chess, medicine, memory, etc.

- Free

There's an excellent book on the topic written by Ericsson and Robert Pool called *Peak: Secrets from the New Science of Expertise*. Dr. Ericsson's kindness and correspondence with me is greatly appreciated. His research can help you (and maybe even me) get on the path to making major improvements.

He's found that purposeful practice is the way to achieve significant performance improvements. It consists of four core components.

1. There must be a specific goal. This provides clarity of focus.

2. The challenge must be addressed with intense focus. Deep thinking and attention to the matter at hand is required.

3. There needs to be immediate feedback. It's important to quickly know the effectiveness of what you're trying. You can't make improvements, if the results of what you're doing are obscured.

4. Frequent occurrences of successes and failures. Having frequent successes and failures by definition means that you're on the edge of what's possible and expanding the envelope of capabilities.

Anders Ericsson's work is where the "10,000 hours to mastery" rule originated before being popularized by Malcolm Gladwell in his book *Outliers: The Story of Success*. Though the rule has often been misinterpreted. As summarized above, just putting in 10,000 hours of practice doesn't necessarily lead to improvement. It's why a physician might be no better at medicine with 25 years of experience, than she is after just 5 years. Same with an athlete or musician (and I'd think executive manager). Contrary to what we've been taught, practice does not make perfect. But "purposeful practice" is the path toward perfection.

There are countless examples of purposeful practice leading to success in the research papers and the book by Ericsson. And there are many historical examples, like the Wright Brothers, where the four core components were clearly applied.

This lesson of purposeful practice is of utmost importance. It's a fundamental principle of how humans learn and improve, and it should be taught to every kid in school. And every person out of school.

Baseball manager Yogi Berra humorously said, "In theory there is no difference between theory and practice. In practice there is."

Turns out, Berra was exactly right. In practice … there is a difference.

Ten Ways to Rewire Your Brain

There were some *amazing* things that happened in the '90s! And one thing in particular that absolutely will expand your mind. Here's the crazy thing … it was overlooked, or forgotten, or maybe suppressed—until recently rediscovered.

But, let's back up a second. Just to make sure we're on the same page, I'm talking about the 1790s. But don't get your pantaloons twisted or flip your powdered wig—this is actually late-breaking news. To show you how groundbreaking this is, let's set the stage with what else was happening in the 1790s.

- President George Washington gives the first State of the Union address.

- The US patent system is established.

- The first blast furnace is constructed by George Anshutz.

- Eli Whitney is granted his patent for the cotton gin.

- Coffee is forbidden by royal decree in Sweden (don't ask me why).

- Mozart creates a prolific amount of music.

- And there's fighting and warring all over the place (some things never seem to change).

Meanwhile, in the 1790s, an Italian anatomist name Michele Vincenzo Malacarne was asked to come up with some experiments to determine if mental exercises could have an impact on the growth of the brain. He came up with a clever experiment.

He took several pairs of brothers and sisters from birth (*not* people, but dogs and birds), and, for a few years, he trained one of the siblings extensively. I'm not sure what the training was, but I am guessing it was learning how to do tricks or remember a path through a maze—and be rewarded with a nice scratch behind the ears and probably some bacon (or whatever Italian dogs and birds enjoyed, maybe salami). Meanwhile, the siblings were allowed to just hang out and do whatever the equivalent was of watching daytime television in the 1790s.

After a few years, Malacarne sacrificed the animals and compared the sibling brains to each other. What he found was astounding. The animals that were trained had larger brains, with more folds, than their untrained siblings. This was big news, as previously nobody thought you could change the physiology of a brain.

His work was so advanced for the times, that it was promptly forgotten and played no part in brain research (albeit little) that happened over the following nearly 200 years.

In fact, during most of the 20th century, scientists believed that the brain was basically a fixed organ, and that its structure was immutable after a critical period of early childhood development. It wasn't until about 1950 that this long-held belief was even challenged by others, including Canadian psychologist Donald Hebb, who has since been described as the father of neural networks.

Work over the past couple of decades now proves the principle of neuroplasticity—basically that your brain is constantly creating new connections and is doing so based on what (and how) you're thinking.

In fact, a study completed in 2005 shows that the human brain rewires faster and more robustly than previously ever imagined. Brain imaging, which was previously not possible, was used in the study. It showed that when medical students studied for their exams, that in a matter of just months their gray matter increased significantly in the posterior and lateral parietal cortex.[2]

It's a shame the work of Malacarne and his animals was forgotten for nearly 200 years!

So, how can you expand your brain and its capacity? Here are ten ways (none have been tested on my dog).

1. Keep Thinking

Learn new things. Struggle to understand new concepts. Maybe that's

why Thomas J. Watson, the founder of IBM, had the simple word
"THINK" on a plaque on his desk. Also, "Use your brain every day, so
it gets better" wouldn't fit.

2. Exercise
   Your brain needs oxygen to function. Getting plenty of oxygen to your
   brain is good.

3. Eat Healthy
   The brain weighs about three pounds. That's just 2 percent of your
   body weight (if you weigh 150 pounds). Yet, amazingly, your brain uses
   20 percent of your resting 1,300 calories used a day. Give yourself, and
   your brain, good nutritious food. Note to self: "Goodbye, Twinkies, I
   shall miss thee."

4. Meditate
   There have been several studies that link meditation to increased
   gray matter, including one from Harvard University.[3] In addition
   to the increase, studies show improvements in a multitude of areas,
   including decreases in anger and sadness, and improved clarity, etc.

5. Be a Lifelong Learner
   Stay curious. Stay interested. Ask "Why?" and, more important, look
   for answers. Stop saying, "I don't know," and go find out. Don't be
   an over-consumer (of content). Be aware of the difference between
   creating content (or art) and consuming content. Sure, it's ok to
   consume some content—to watch the game, or some news, or a
   favorite show. But according to a report from Nielsen, the average
   American watches more than five hours of television per day.[4] That's
   frightening.

6. Be Creative
   Sir Ken Robinson, an internationally recognized leader in education
   and business, says, "Creativity is putting your imagination to work,
   and it's produced the most extraordinary results in human culture."
   Yea, not only that … it makes your brain stronger. Take some
   photographs, learn an instrument, make a collage of whatever it is you
   like, write a letter or a story. Go create.

7. Enjoy Music
   If you've not yet seen the 2014 documentary *Alive Inside*—you should

watch it. It's excellent. Get started by watching the trailer.[5] It shows how music remains alive in parts of the brain that are essentially untouched by the ravages of Alzheimer's. Go put some beautiful music (whatever that is to you) into your brain. It'll always be a part of you.

8. Drink Water
   Your brain is 75 percent water. It functions and you think through chemicals and electrical impulses traveling at unimaginable speeds. Best to provide a clean medium.

9. Get Your Rest
   Just because scientists don't know a lot about sleep, doesn't mean you don't know why it's important. Even as an experiment of one— *you* know this for sure. You think better when you're rested, when the restorative powers of sleep allow your brain to work its magic. Rewire, store, dream, remix, whatever. Let your brain do its best by letting it sleep.

10. Love
    I'm adding this tenth way without the benefit of a clinical study, or any advanced molecular, cellular, or brain-imaging studies. I'm just going to flat out tell you what my brain is thinking … it needs love to function at its best. The chemicals of dopamine, phenylethylamine, norepinephrine, oxytocin, and serotonin are released when we love. They stimulate thinking and that will make you feel all tingly and connected to each other and the universe.

In closing, my brain wants to wish your brain well. Despite our outward appearances, we're really much (much) more similar than dissimilar. Regardless of what's on the outside, it's what's on the inside that matters. Let's continue to think and grow.

Yes or No?

The first time John Lennon saw his future wife was at an art exhibit. The Beatle walked in to a local art gallery in London and took a look around. One of the art pieces was an installation by an artist named Yoko Ono. Her installation involved a wooden ladder, the kind you might get out of the garage when you need to change a light bulb on the porch, or maybe reach some apples in a tree. On top of the ladder, she mounted a spyglass. Visitors to the art exhibit were able to climb up the few steps of the ladder and see what was visible through the lens.

John was curious, so he climbed the ladder and looked. He later described that what he saw made an immediate and positive impression on him.

Which naturally reminds me of an executive meeting I attended. As with many meetings, there were too many people. Probably thirteen from the client side, and the president of the company and me from my side, trying to sell something.

The meeting was not going well. The president was knowledgeable, confident, and articulate. He was also exceedingly verbose. He talked. A lot.

Here's the rundown. The client would ask a simple question. The president would use it as an opportunity to regale them with a rambling story, leading (sometimes) to the answer. A few times, he forgot the question and had to ask for a reminder. Sometimes the client had to ask again.

Simple question. "Does your product allow for various user rights and permissions?"

Rambling answer. "Back when we first started thinking about the feature set to offer …" (minutes later). "What was your question again?"

It was frustrating. My mind wandered, and I turned my head from the room to look out through the large windows. Outside, the lights from Times Square were glowing brightly many stories below. Everywhere I looked, there were lights, and the streets were buzzing with people. On a nearby high-rise, there was a huge LCD screen that covered the entire side of the building. The giant screen was several stories tall. One of the things it was playing was a promotional advertisement for some upcoming basketball tournament, or maybe it was a new athletic shoe. I don't remember.

But I do remember the five-second clip of the basketball player catching the ball, and then the fluid motion of him jumping into the air and slamming it through the basket, before a quick cut to the cheering fans. Every few minutes it would repeat.

That wasn't happening in the meeting. What my boss was doing was catching the ball (those simple easy questions being tossed to him from the client) and then dribbling back and forth (uninterrupted) on the court, sometimes going nearer the basket, seemingly about to take the shot, only to move away from the basket and dribble some more. If the questions were like basketballs, he'd spin each one on his fingers or dribble the ball between his legs (he was really knowledgeable). Eventually, most of the time, he would put the ball into the basket.

I stopped looking out the window. The meeting dragged on. The client grew increasingly impatient with the long-winded responses.

A few hours later, sitting in a Starbucks with the president of my company, I tried to explain my take on the meeting and how things could be improved the next time. "Think of yourself as a star basketball player, and the questions are passed to you like a ball," I said.

Associating him with a star athlete seemed to align with his opinion of himself. He leaned forward. Maybe he was imagining himself on the floor of Madison Square Garden.

"In the future, just take the question and immediately make the basket." His eyes widened. "Don't make them wait and wonder when you'll ever get around to the answer. The question has been passed to you to answer. So just answer 'yes' or 'no.'" At this point, he nodded his head in understanding and was likely envisioning himself in a Knicks jersey.

"Once you've done that, you can add some additional explanation, but everyone is waiting for you to make the basket, so they can move on to the next question. The objective is to quickly answer the questions and score the points, not to see you do tricks." He smiled as though he could hear the crowd's thunderous approval after dunking an imaginary basket.

Constructive criticism isn't always easy, but the explanation seemed to go well.

So, what did Lennon see when he climbed the ladder and looked through the spyglass? Inside the lens, Yoko Ono had put the word "YES."

John said that at the time, the world seemed to be full of negativity and that most concept art was "anti" everything. So naturally, he expected to see something cynical. Instead, that one simple direct word of affirmation touched his sensibilities.

Said another way ... maybe John Lennon had a question and cheered when he got a direct answer.

Thoughts on Life and Happiness

Thomas Jefferson was dying. It was early July in 1826, and Jefferson had been in and out of consciousness for days. He was clearly struggling to remain alive until the Fourth of July. On the morning of July 4 (50 years to the day after signing the Declaration of Independence) Jefferson's grandson quietly walked into his grandfather's bedroom and whispered into his ear that the day was the fourth of July. Shortly thereafter, Jefferson took his last breath.

Of all the accolades, one of the best compliments about Thomas Jefferson was made by President John Kennedy on April 29, 1962. That evening, there was a dinner at the White House honoring the Nobel Prize winners of the Western hemisphere. There were a lot of smart guests attending—including 46 US citizens, one Canadian, one Frenchman, one German, and other prominent men and women from the arts, education, and sciences—including presidents from several universities.

At the beginning of his welcoming remarks, President Kennedy said to the group, "I think this is the most extraordinary collection of talent, of human knowledge, that has ever been gathered at the White House—with the possible exception of when Thomas Jefferson dined alone."[6]

Jefferson was, of course, an American Founding Father, the principle author of the Declaration of Independence, the third US president and founder of the University of Virginia (at 76 years of age). He was a lifelong learner—reader, writer, astronomer, architect, paleontologist (he has a mammoth named after him, musician—and curious innovator. He was the first commissioner and inspector of patents for the United States.

Here are some of my favorite quotes from Jefferson.

"Do you want to know who you are? Don't ask.
Act! Action will delineate and define you."

"Determine never to be idle ...
It is wonderful how much may be done if we are always doing."

By definition, progress means moving forward, and throughout his 83 years, Jefferson exhibited a massive bias for action.

"The variety of opinions leads to questions.
Questions lead to truth."

This reminds me of a tenet from lean/agile/scrum methodology to always be maximizing opportunities for feedback. Continual improvements are made through the opinions and input from the team. (As an aside, there were a lot of similarities the Founding Fathers had while hammering out the Declaration of Independence with a scrum team; they were cross-functional, self-directing, self-organizing, and reviewed the work at various sprint cycles.)

"Nothing can stop the man with the right
mental attitude from achieving his goal.

Nothing on earth can help the man with the wrong mental attitude."

Nothing to add here.

"He who knows best knows how little he knows."

For all his knowing, Jefferson kept an attitude of humbleness. There's a term in Japanese martial arts and Zen Buddhism called "shoshin," which means having a "beginner's mind." It entails having an appreciation for how much there is to learn, for openness, and for acknowledging that there's always more to learn.

"Always take hold of things by the smooth handle."

This could be interpreted in different ways, but to me, it simply means to deal with things in a dignified and reputable (and the easiest) manner.

"The man who reads nothing at all is better educated
than the man who reads nothing but newspapers."

Jefferson was referring to the short-sighted, trivial, and gossipy nature of much of what was printed in the newspapers in the late 1700s. Or maybe he was making a prediction as to much of what's in newspapers and on the internet today.

"I like the dreams of the future better than the history of the past."

As evidenced by all he accomplished, the man was always looking forward.

"A little rebellion now and then is a good thing."

Jefferson was not beyond criticism and knew firsthand the trials and tribulations (and inertia) that go along with affecting change.

"The glow of one warm thought is to me worth more than money."

Thomas Jefferson was a man who valued ideas. To give his comment some perspective, think about the fact that the Declaration of Independence was the blueprint for the United States and a guide for democracy around the world. No doubt a thought is worth more than money.

Rules for Creating Your Future (from a Rock Guitarist)

I came across a couple of interviews that I found to be insightful for anyone wanting to create and improve an extraordinary business or life. What's noteworthy is that the interviews were with someone from an area not typically associated with teaching leadership or growth. The interviews were with rock guitar virtuoso Steve Vai.

Now, you might think a guitar slinger's experiences probably don't have a lot of applicability to your product development, marketing efforts, or crisis-of-the-day at work—however, you'd be wrong. In fact, listening to Steve Vai's words of wisdom, I couldn't help but think of how Peter Drucker, the preeminent business educator, responded to the question of how to become a better manager. He simply replied, "Learn how to play the violin." [7]

You might or might not know Steve Vai's music, but he is a unique and talented guitar player, and his profound and timeless words of advice are also worth a listen. Steve spoke and answered questions during a private session for guitar players in Hollywood, California. He was separately interviewed by another guitar player and teacher, Justin Sandercoe, to talk shop.[8]

What struck me throughout the interviews is how absolutely candid Steve was concerning what he believes are the fundamental reasons for his success. Without a hint of sarcasm or overinflated ego, Steve described his early fears and his thoughtful advice about what it takes to succeed.

Here is a summary of his advice.

1. Do What You Love

   Steve Vai starts out by saying how he's always been in love with the guitar, and how even in a world of distractions, it got him to focus on improving. In fact, Steve acquired a sense of achievement, simply from each small improvement he was able to make with the instrument. During the interview, he gives an offhand, yet Zen-like, comment explaining why he values improvement—"The better you get, the better you get." Simple and true.

2. Be Original

   As is the case for any artist creating original work, Steve said it always felt weird to play somebody else's music. "They [the original musicians] do it so much better." As for why he preferred creating his own music, he said, "How cool is it to do things you haven't heard before." This desire to do more than mimic others led him to develop his unique talent and create his own music.

3. Conquer Your Fear and Create What You Want

   Hard to imagine for a guitar player who's toured the world and played with some of the greatest musical artists, but Steve talks about his childhood fear of performing, and how the thought of playing the guitar in front of people would keep him awake at night. So, rather than continuing to be plagued by fear, Steve would put on his headphones and while listening to all his favorite music, he would create this image of himself playing the guitar in front of a lot of people, and playing with complete confidence from head to toe and in total command of the instrument.

   He pictured himself as this enigmatic figure and imagined himself playing completely elegantly and effortlessly, in a manner that was almost unseen or unheard of. "I was never pretentious enough to actually think that I could play like that. But that was the picture I created, and you perpetuate your own reality." No surprise that a lot of what Steve does now is a direct reflection of what he imagined as a kid.

4. Practice Your Craft

   As with most virtuosos, Steve Vai is known for mind-boggling amounts of time spent meticulously practicing his craft. In the interview, he's asked about an article he'd written for a guitar magazine wherein he talks about his ten-hour daily practice sessions. Casually, Steve explains, "It was a lot more than ten hours actually," and that the ten-hour practice session was just what he'd put in the magazine at the time. He goes on to say that for him, playing the guitar was never about work. His advice to guitar students, "Pick a time and turn off the distractions."

5. Focus on Your Strengths
   Steve says he never worked on his weaknesses; but rather he only worked on his strengths—and then, he exaggerated them. Everyone has particular natural talents, and the best thing to do is focus on developing those. When you get discouraged, go back to the big picture. Improvement is an ongoing process.

6. Don't Worry about What You Might Be Missing
   When asked whether he missed out on doing other things, Steve explains, "When you're absorbed in something, you don't miss anything." He goes on to say, "Whenever I wasn't playing the guitar, I was in pain. Everything else was boring. Everything else was work." That sounds like a true artist.

7. Find Your Own Way
   While Steve built his skill and capabilities by relentlessly practicing and methodically transcribing complex musical notations (he transcribed Frank Zappa's music), he knows that what worked for him might not work for somebody else. Steve's way was being methodical, but he explains, "The way for you is what you feel. If you're going to take any advice from me, it's to find what excites you the most and go after that. Find what excites you and disregard what others are doing or saying." It takes a real visionary to advise you to have faith in yourself and ignore others—even him.

8. It's All in Your Thoughts
   Steve Vai comes right out and says that the only thing that holds you back is your thoughts, and explains that "the level of achievement that we have at anything is a reflection of how well we were able to focus on it."

At the end of one of the interviews, Justin Sandercoe asked Steve how long he had to play the guitar until he felt that he was able to express himself through the instrument. Steve's answer is classic and right on. With just a moment's thought, he replied, "Always and never." Steve went on to explain that the moment you pick up an instrument, you're expressing yourself to a degree; but that he still always feels like it's an ongoing process.

Trying to come at the question from a slightly different perspective, Justin, who is obviously a great admirer of Steve Vai, follows up by asking, "But you must be able to play anything you can hear, right?" Steve replies, matter of factly, "Well, no." Steve adds that he's always taking himself to the brink of his potential, and a regular exercise he does is to imagine things that he can't do, and then he visualizes himself doing them. "And like magic it starts to happen. And once you accomplish that, there's no end."

The Biggest Fight of Your Life

Invention or creation is rarely easy. That's true if you're innovating within an industry or reinventing yourself. Your success is never assured. The vast majority of time, your efforts take place unseen and are never fully appreciated. Many people get started; some drop off along the way. Most reach a modicum of success and then their drive levels off for understandable reasons.

A smaller few stay the course and continue pushing further ahead. Because it feels like it's what they were born to do. And because they often feel like they have no choice but to pursue their calling.

We typically think this is the realm of artists, poets, musicians, and entertainers. They labor for the love of what they do and possibly for the chance to wildly succeed. But it's also the realm of anyone—teachers, engineers, mechanics, or chefs—who puts themselves on the path to mastery and fights to keep themselves there.

Manny Pacquiao has been on the path to mastery for much of his life. He's come a long way, and he has some words relevant to the fight in your life.

*"I remember as a little boy I ate one meal a day and sometimes
slept in the street. I will never forget that, and it inspires*

me to fight hard, stay strong and remember all the people of
my country, trying to achieve better for themselves."

Manny Pacquiao was raised in the Philippines and lived with his mother and five siblings in extreme poverty. He left home when he was 14 years old and moved to Manila. He struggled. He sold donuts. The first time he fought, he made $1 and gave it to his mother.

He started his professional boxing career when he was 16 years old. Weighing only 98 pounds, he was under the weight requirement, so he loaded his pockets at the weigh-in.

"I wanted to be a world champion."

Manny Pacquiao had a seemingly impossible goal from the most unlikely of beginnings. For some reason, he thought he could be world champion. He went on to win ten world titles.

"Life is meant to be a challenge, because challenges make you grow."

True. Exactly.

"All those who are around me are the bridge to
my success, so they are all important."

Whatever your path, remember that along with years of woodshedding, it takes a team of people working together to effect change. The myth of the lone inventor, or the self-made success, is just that.

"I'm just a regular person who believes life is
simple, and I like a simple life."

Here's the thing, we're mostly all "regular people" and what's more, life is simple. That's not to say people don't aggrandize their importance or confound themselves with complexity.

Do your best and do good along the way. Simple.

"I can be a champion and a public servant also."

Pacquiao served two terms as a member of Congress in the Philippines (2010–2016) and is now a senator.

"I consider myself a student of boxing, a philosopher so to speak, and my philosophy is to keep learning."

Continually learning and growing is necessary to remain competitive. That's true if your work is weaving and jabbing or if it's technology and business.

"Boxing is not about your feelings. It's about performance."

Doing great work matters, but so does accomplishing what you set out to do. Get your work out into the world. Suffer the bumps and bruises, learn and evolve.

"It's just a game. Sometimes you win, sometimes you lose."

Manny Pacquiao had what was arguably the biggest fight of his life on May 2, 2015, against Floyd Mayweather Jr. Pacquiao lost.

In the end, it's a game. Or it's work. It's what we do, it's not who we are.

Who are we? Sons or daughters, fathers or mothers, friends, neighbors, colleagues. We're innovators, business people, or artists. And we're on to the next fight in our lives.

Be That One

You'll likely figure out the ending of this story long before I did.

Several years ago, I was in Newark, New Jersey, for an afternoon meeting. I had just parked my car in a parking lot when I caught the eye of a man who appeared to be somewhat distressed. He quickly walked over to me, explaining that someone had stolen the battery from his car, and he needed another $20 to buy a new battery so he could get home. He was holding jumper cables, so I figured he must have initially thought his battery was dead. He looked stuck.

So, I gave him $20 and was happy to help out.

> *"There's a sucker born every minute."*
> —Attributed (incorrectly) to P. T. Barnum

I remember just a few things from history class in high school. One of them was the day our teacher, an enthusiastic man with black curly hair, brought goldfish to the classroom when we were discussing the 1950s. There were a lot of important events we discussed about the decade, the least of which was the goldfish-swallowing craze.

But, one of the things I vividly remember (actually, I can see it *right now* as this is being written) was our teacher reaching into the bowl, grabbing a live goldfish, and dangling the squirming fish above his mouth—before letting it fall. And then him looking at the class with his cheeks puffed out, before … actually swallowing the fish!

Keep in mind, this was in rural Indiana. Either sushi wasn't yet invented, or it hadn't made its way across the cornfields.

I also remember a story about Thomas Jefferson, one of our Founding Fathers.

Jefferson and several other men were traveling by horseback through rural northern Virginia during a winter evening. It was a cold, harsh evening. The horsemen were riding single file along the trail, approaching the point of crossing a stream on their horses.

As they approached the stream, they could see an elderly man in the dark alongside the trail, who stared silently as each of the men on horseback passed him by. As the last rider in the group was passing, the old man looked into the eyes of the horseman and asked for a ride across, explaining that there didn't appear to be any other way to cross without getting wet.

This last horseman was, of course, Thomas Jefferson, who happily agreed to provide a ride. Jefferson dismounted his horse and helped the nearly freezing old man onto the horse. Not only did Jefferson take the man across the river, but he also continued riding some distance to take the old man to his destination.

As Jefferson helped the old man down from the horse, he asked the man why he waited until the last horseman was passing before asking for help, as surely that left only one remaining chance of being taken across the stream.

The old man, who did not recognize Jefferson, explained that he'd seen a lot in life, and that when he looked into the faces of the other men, he saw little empathy and therefore felt his request would fall on deaf ears. But when he looked into the face of Jefferson, he saw kindness, compassion, and empathy.

That story resonated with me and made me always want to have that kind of face. To be that one.

Of course, sometimes it doesn't work out, or you get tricked. But the good outcomes probably greatly outweigh the costs. That's what I tell myself.

So, fast forward back to the future. It was exactly one week after I helped the man with the stolen battery, when I was back in Newark for a follow-up meeting and parked in the same parking lot.

And I swear … to … you … as I was walking through the parking lot, the *same* man who I'd given money to the prior week, *also* happened to be there at the same time. He sees me, nods his head to get my attention, and walks over to me, smiling.

You might have guessed that the man recognized me, insisted on paying me back, and that we've been friends and colleagues ever since. Turns out he was the chairman of a $3 billion company and happened to be in need of senior marketing/business development executive. That small act of kindness and coincidental meeting resulted in my joining his company and enjoying many years of friendship and business success.

But that's not what happened.

What actually happened, is that he walked up to me and said, "Excuse me, sir. Somebody just stole the battery from my car, and I just need $20 more so I can buy a new one."

Here's how I look at it. I might be an easy mark, but that's a small cost for having a kind, compassionate (and perhaps naïve) face.

"At fifty, every man has the face he deserves."
—George Orwell

Love Over Gold

I reread the article in the *New York Times*, titled "For the Love of Money," by Sam Polk,[9] wherein he wrote about his being addicted to money (among other harmful substances). Mr. Polk worked on Wall Street as a bond and credit default swap trader. He discussed being disappointed making only $1.5 million in his second year at the hedge fund, and then a few years later, while just 30 years old, being unhappy with a $3.6 million bonus. In 2010, Mr. Polk quit his job, after demanding $8 million instead of $3.6 million.

In the article, Mr. Polk talked about something he described as the addiction to money. He seemed quite candid in revealing his own addictions and shortcomings and gave credit to hard work and his counselor for helping him make changes. While Sam Polk took a critical look at himself, he also described a wealth addict's distorted perspective. As an example, he mentioned McDonald's CEO Don Thompson, whose compensation in 2012 was $14 million—including an $8.5 million bonus—the same year his company published a financial guide for its low-wage employees offering advice how to survive on low pay. The guide presumed that workers should have a second full-time job (and no heating bill).

While it seems crazy for anyone in Mr. Polk's shoes (likely expensive and new) to be angry about a $3.8 million bonus, I'm not passing judgment. The world is full of several billion people, from all walks of life. What's more, there has nearly always been huge differences in wealth.

But the article did have me thinking about choices people make, and what makes for a meaningful work life. We might not always be able to do exactly what we want in our work lives, but it's probably a worthwhile exercise to think about what is meaningful to us as individuals.

Here is a start at what meaningful work includes (for me).

- The desire to be involved with innovation. Innovation and technology contain the promise of doing things better and faster, of leveraging human capability (bulldozers increase our physical capability, computers leverage our mental capabilities).

- Improve the world. Yes, it sounds corny … but it could be argued that everything we do makes a difference. With that in mind, we're either improving and contributing (being a good parent, volunteering to pick up some trash in our town, holding a door for someone), or we're not (forwarding more erroneous, fear-based emails; doing nothing). Sure, there's a theoretical neutral line, but my guess is you're either adding to the good, or you're not.

- Working alongside great people. Great people not only make it happen, but you can't help but learn and improve with them as your colleagues. These folks have characteristics that include being knowledgeable, collaborative, inquisitive, genuine, hardworking, value-driven, creative, generous, thoughtful, striving, open-minded, and having an abundance mentality.

- Personal growth. Humans are designed to learn and grow. Learning feels good and is empowering.

- An opportunity to contribute. Everybody wants to have helped move the needle—whether it's the calculations that went into cooling the circuit board, the driveline installation instructions, or an element of the product launch campaign. Everybody wants to have helped.

- An opportunity to teach. In addition to being natural learners, we all have something to teach. Everybody is an expert at something. Help those around you.

- Being on the team. Sure, we're each individuals. But it feels good to be a part of a team, to be a contributing colleague, to collaborate wholeheartedly. Don't hold back, be a part of the whole. And yes, it's best when the whole is greater than the sum of the parts.

- Making a difference. Steve Jobs called Apple's huge attempts at product innovation … "making a dent in the universe." Even if your work is not that far reaching, it still matters that you're intent on bettering things, on doing what hasn't been done before, on making a difference.

- Work hard. This might seem a bit counterintuitive, but working hard is meaningful because it is necessary for clearing every major hurdle. Hard work moves the seemingly unmovable. It's what results in new products, improves operating efficiencies, and creates a demonstrable sales tool that wows. It's what drives revenue.

I could probably come up with a few more … but money hasn't even yet made the list.

You Won the Lottery!

It's often impolite to talk about winning, especially where luck is involved, like the lottery. And I get that. Although people love to play the lottery, that's evidenced by the $70 billion Americans spend on lottery tickets each year. That's far more than the $18 billion spent on sports tickets or the $11 billion spent going to the movies.

And every lottery ticket is bought by someone hoping to win. Everybody wants to win, and they imagine what it must be like to find out. Here's what I *imagine* it would be like.

It was from a phone call one evening in the middle of a typical week. When I heard my wife's voice, I knew within milliseconds something profound had happened. Her voice was trembling; she said she checked the numbers four times before calling. Shots of electricity pulsed through me. I felt disoriented.

It was in the evening; everyone else in the office had already left so there was no one to tell. Not that I would have anyway. For one thing, it's private. For another, my hands were shaking and I was perspiring.

I do not remember driving home, but I do vividly recall being greeted at the front door as though I was an astronaut returning home from a historic mission to Mars. We methodically confirmed the numbers. It's easy, the same numbers are used every time—13 for my mom's birthday, 3 for my dad's birthday (he'll be the first one I call later that evening), 22 for our daughter, 30 for our son, 9 for my wife's birthday, and 1 for me (I was born on the first of the month). The numbers match.

And maybe due to some minor obsession remaining from childhood, or maybe because I'm feeling delirious and need some grounding, I say, "Let's just check again 10 times." And that's what we do, and each time my wife makes a check on a scrap of paper. Confirmed. Confirmed. Confirmed … 10 times.

The first call is to my dad, who's nearly 70 years old at the time. He's worked for nearly 55 years. I start by saying, "Dad, you are a winner."

I learn later, when you pick 6 numbers from a pool of 49 numbers, your chances of winning the New Jersey jackpot are 1 in 13,983,816. That's 1 shot in almost 14 million.

Statistics and probabilities can be difficult to comprehend, so here's an accurate comparison. If you had one pet turtle—the size of a laptop computer—that roamed in a pen that was one mile long by a half mile wide (that's 14 million square feet), and one day you were flying in a helicopter over the property and you randomly threw out a Frisbee, and it landed directly on top of that turtle … that would be 1 in 14 million.

It seems really unlikely, but clearly it happens. And that got me curious about other probabilities, of things that are happening all around us. For example, do you know what the odds are for each of us being born? It's easy to determine, I found a study from the Massachusetts Institute of Technology (MIT) that explained a fertile woman has 100,000 viable eggs, on average. A man produces 12 trillion sperm over the course of his reproductive life. The probability of the right sperm meeting the right egg (to create you) is 1 in 400 quadrillion (that's a 400, with 15 zeros).

If even one different sperm met one different egg, you would not be reading this.

That probability is certainly difficult to comprehend, so here's an accurate example. If you consider the surface area of *all* the oceans in all the world (70 percent of Earth) … and if you had just one little pet turtle with about a one-inch shell—and that little turtle was swimming somewhere (anywhere) on the surface of any ocean anywhere in the world (which is about 400 quadrillion square inches), and one day you were flying in your jet on a transoceanic flight and you dropped a single postage stamp, and it floated down through the clouds, and it landed on the back of *that* turtle … that would be 1 in 400 quadrillion.

And that puts the far more likely odds of winning the New Jersey lottery in perspective.

Which brings us back to where I began, when I *imagined* what it would be like to win the lottery.

Now, the reality is, I did *not* win the New Jersey or any state lottery. I've actually never bought a lottery ticket. This was just an imagined scenario, as described above.

But both of us did win—the far more valuable and unimaginably impossible odds of being born, of being here. Each of us won that lottery. Invest your time and resources wisely!

One, Two, Three, Four (Drum Intro)

We've all turned up the stereo and blasted a favorite song. And loudly sang along. And probably danced alone in the living room. Maybe even played a little air guitar.

We call singers, songwriters, and musicians "musical artists" for a reason. Their work, their art, can inspire us. Immediately put us in a better mood. Change our attitude.

And, as with any work of art, it's personal to each of us. You might be moved by Beethoven's Symphony No. 4. For someone else (me, for example) it would be Bruce Springsteen's "Born to Run." The music is different. Yet, to each of us, it's truly amazing art.

Most people probably don't think of their own work as art. The standard thinking goes—whether you're an engineer, homemaker, marketer, or teacher—aren't you just doing a job? The answer is—hopefully—no.

Certainly many of the folks at Apple, Nike, Tesla Motors, Amazon, and countless other companies (big and small) think they're doing work that matters a great deal. They take their work seriously. They are changing the world with their craft. The first words in the Wikipedia article for the word "Art" state, "Art is a diverse range of human activities ... these activities include the production of ... art."[10]

When you strive to do your best work, you're creating art. You might not have considered that before. And thinking of your work as your "art" probably seems aggrandizing and even a little disconcerting. After all, it probably isn't great (yet). But, it is your art.

And with practice (a lot of practice), your "art" might have an impact on others. So keep honing your craft and practicing your art—whatever it is. Most important, strive to do great work. Your fans are waiting for your next masterpiece.

How September 11 Broke My Heart and What I Try to Remember

I was in the World Trade Center less than a dozen hours before the attack on September 11, 2001.

For years I commuted in and out of New York City, and each day I'd be in the World Trade Center in the morning and the evening. Usually my commute would have me driving partway, and then taking the Port Authority Trans-Hudson (PATH) train into the World Trade Center. Occasionally, I'd drive partway and take the ferry across the Hudson River, which would let off its passengers adjacent to the World Trade Center.

On several occasions, either heading into the city or coming home in the evening, I would cross paths with a neighbor from the small New Jersey town where we both lived. He was much admired by my family and me. When my daughter was a young girl, he was her first soccer coach, and he set the watermark for what a coach should be. She played for probably another ten years on traveling and high school teams, yet his name was always invoked as the best example of patience, encouragement, and kindness. My son, who was a little boy at the time, was enamored with the coach's Land Rover, and, in fact, my boy had his own toy Land Rover Matchbox version.

Normally, I was content to commute to the city in silence, probably thinking about (sometimes dreading) the work to be done. But on the days my neighbor and I crossed paths, we always enjoyed each other's company and would spend the time talking about life and family. Occasionally, we drove together from our town.

There is one occasion that I often think about. Despite it being a cold and blustery New Jersey day, we thought it'd be fun to take the ferry. After boarding, we climbed the stairs to the open-air upper deck. The morning air was freezing. There was just one other person outside with us, though he stood close to the wheelhouse to shield himself from the harsh wind.

We walked to the stern of the ferry, where we'd get a better view of the skyline, and stood alongside the white railing. Squinting from the morning light reflecting off the choppy water, we stood quietly in the cutting wind and watched the city grow closer, our eyes watering from the wind. I was wearing a knit hat and remember thinking maybe his head wasn't cold because of all his hair.

We walked into the World Trade Center before going our separate ways. For me, it meant heading outside to continue walking to an office a few blocks down the street on Broadway, while my friend would make his way to the bank of elevators to head up into the tower.

The night of September 10, I worked late and was the last person to leave the office. It was approaching 11 p.m. The World Trade Center was nearly empty, as I made my way down the stairs and escalators to catch the PATH train to Harrison, New Jersey, where my car was parked.

The next morning, on September 11, rather than immediately heading out to the city, for some reason I grabbed my guitar and sat down to play. Perhaps subconsciously, I felt like taking some time in light of the previous late night in the office. An hour later, I was still playing when the phone rang. It was a panicked call from a friend checking on my whereabouts. What he told me didn't make sense. I remember thinking, *How in the world could a pilot fly into the tower?*

Like millions of people around the world, I turned on the television and stood in slack-jawed disbelief. Later that morning, I walked through the woods in town, up to the top of a hill to look the twenty-some miles toward the city. I watched the smoke rising.

It would be impossible to express how sad I was about the loss of my friend and the heartbreak his family had to endure.

We weren't allowed to go back to our offices for several weeks, instead I worked from client offices in midtown. Eventually, we had a police escort into our building, so we could retrieve our laptops and personal items.

Several weeks later, we were allowed to return to our building, and for the next several months I watched the reclamation of Ground Zero. Endless trips of trucks removing twisted metal and concrete.

For years, 9/11 was on my mind. The evil that caused the event bewildered me. There was a lot of sorrow, melancholy, and confusion. Many of my friends expressed feeling the same way, and I suspect millions of others did too.

In the end, I try to think about these ideas.

- The great everyday heroes who made their presence known.

- The good lives lost and remembered.

- The millions of people around the world who showed their support.

- The belief that inevitably wisdom and love triumph over ignorance and hate.

In the end, and in no small way, what eventually began to displace my anger and sadness was the image of my neighbor coaching the little kids on the soccer field, smiling and offering shouts of encouragement. And the image of him standing in the cold air on the top deck of the ferry; the dawn's first rays lighting the city, and him facing into the wind.

The Multitasking Myth

Dr. Earl Miller is a smart guy, and he can teach you something really important about your brain. What he knows will definitely improve your career and your life, and could even save a life. And, if you've got a few seconds, there's a cool little experiment you can do to demonstrate this to yourself.

But I'm getting ahead of myself; let me introduce you to him.

Earl Miller received his doctoral degree in psychology and neuroscience from Princeton University. He has been the Picower Professor of Neuroscience at the Picower Institute for Learning and Memory and the Department of Brain and Cognitive Sciences at the Massachusetts Institute of Technology (MIT) since 1995.

Professor Miller has spent decades conducting important research on the brain and has been the recipient of a variety of awards for his illuminating work. In brief, his work has helped show that the human brain does not think about more than one thing at a time.

"Tom, your brain is single task." I thought he might be spying on me, but then he added, "Everyone's brain is single task." I breathed a sigh of relief; thank goodness he's been spying on everyone's brain.

Here's how Dr. Miller knows this about the brain. He and his colleagues have studied how the brain actually works by having people think about different problems, while those same people were having their brains imaged.

Dr. Miller explained that the way the brain actually works is that it switches quickly from focusing on one task to another. He explains, "You're not paying attention to one or two things simultaneously, but switching between them very rapidly."[11]   And there's real inefficiency in having to remember where you were each time you approach either task.

He gives an example of what many of us do all too often—writing an email while talking on the phone at the same time. You might think you're actively engaged with both tasks, but the reality is that you're only focused and working on one at a time. "You cannot focus on one while doing the other."

"People can't multitask very well," Dr. Miller said. And interestingly, his research shows that people who think they're good at multitasking are actually the worst. "The brain is very good at deluding itself."

It's certainly easy to fall into the trap of trying to do two (or more) things at once. With a nearly constant stream of emails, ringing phones, meetings, hallway conversations, people dropping by with urgent questions; not to mention social media and news access—it's no wonder we end up trying to multitask.

But the research shows that multitasking always results in the tasks taking longer to complete than if they were completed one at a time. In addition to taking longer, multitasking often results in mistakes, which cause new problems and even greater delays. Said another way, "Multitasking means screwing up several things at once."

Sometimes the mistakes are minor, such as inadvertently including the wrong person in an email. Other times, the mistakes can be huge. I don't know if multitasking contributed to NASA using the metric system to build a satellite while its partner Lockheed Martin used the English system. But the oversight caused the $125-million satellite to be lost in space.[12]   Undoubtedly, these were smart people working hard on innumerable complex issues.

I asked Dr. Miller what we could do to improve our thinking, and he gave these suggestions.

1. Plan to focus. In other words, set aside a time of the day when you will be heads-down thinking.

2. Remove distractions. Consider turning off the mobile phone, closing down the internet, or putting a "Do Not Disturb" sign on your door.

3. Take a break. When you're tired and your thinking is no longer productive, be sure to give your brain a rest or shift focus.

I promised Dr. Miller to include a mention of something important, and that is the danger of using a phone while driving. He stressed a few times to me during the conversation that research shows people miss about 50 percent of things while simultaneously driving and talking on the phone.

And that is even true with a hands-free phone set. It's simply a matter of how the human brain works. Language requires brainpower, and engaging in conversation requires focus. The admonishment from Dr. Miller (who knows how we think) is, "Do not talk on the phone while driving."

Interestingly, having a conversation with another person in the car is not as dangerous, because that other passenger is in sync with traffic and weather demands. The individual can actually act as another set of eyes—while a person on the phone is oblivious to such matters.

So, what about that cool little experiment I mentioned to show that your brain can only "think" about one thing at a time? (Note: Of course, you can learn to do more than one thing at a time, like walking and juggling, but Dr. Miller's work is concerned with critical thinking.)

While sitting, lift your right leg a few inches off the floor and move your foot in a clockwise circular motion. While continuing to move your foot in a clockwise circle, put your right hand in the air and trace the number six.

Did you notice what happened? Your foot reversed its motion and moved counterclockwise.

I tried this a few times and each time ended with my rotating my foot in the wrong direction. I'm glad this didn't involve calculating trajectory paths for satellites.

Lessons to Teach Your Children

They say lightning never strikes the same place twice. But, I've been struck twice by lightning. It changed my life, and although I don't think about it every day, I certainly should. It makes me feel like one of the luckiest people alive.

Well, when I say, "struck by lightning," I mean a metaphorical bolt. Here's what happened.

One fall day in California, twenty some years ago, I'd woken up just before dawn. My daughter, who was about three years old at the time, typically would wake up shortly after sunrise, so thinking this was a good opportunity to let my wife sleep in (for a change), I walked down the hallway and sat down on the floor outside my daughter's bedroom door. I didn't want to wake her early, so I leaned against the wall and watched her sleeping in the crib.

As the first rays of light were just starting to lighten her room, she slowly began to move. In a few minutes, she'd kicked off the blanket, sat up, and was quietly talking to herself. It was like music to me. I stayed hidden in the hallway, watching and listening to her. I remember being completely filled with awe and love.

She had no idea I was watching her. Eventually she climbed out of her crib and walked to her bedroom window and moved the drape aside. Looking outside at the sunlight starting to light the day, she said out loud, "Oh, wow."

Zap! That was the first lightning strike. It was the sound of sublime enchantment. I remember feeling like I'd witnessed something rare. A child's awe of the day that lay ahead.

Several years later, while living in New Jersey, I'd again woken up just before dawn. My son at this point was about three years old.

And yes, the story is exactly the same. I was sitting outside his bedroom door, waiting for him to wake up so we could start the day and let his mom get some needed rest. Eventually, he woke up, climbed out of his crib, went to his window, and looked outside at the fall day. He said (I swear to you) the exact same words out loud, "Oh, wow."

Flash! That was the second lightning strike. It was once again the sound of wonder, and once again it felt like I was observing a child's pure joy for the world outside the window.

At this point, both of my kids are young adults. My son is in college and my daughter graduated a few years ago. Of course, I've learned a lot of things by being their dad; beginning with how they greeted the day many years ago. And over the years, I've tried to teach them some things too.

Here are 25 concepts, in no particular order, that my wife and I told our kids over the years. I'm not sure how many took root, but if repetition counts … believe me, there's a good shot.

1. Put down you smartphone.

    The phone isn't making you smarter. Actually, it's slowly draining your attention from more important things (even noticing the clouds) through constant pings that have conditioned many of your peers (certainly not you) into a knee-jerk immediacy of constantly checking. Don't let the technology (or habituated communication) control you.

2. Learn to say "no."

    This might actually be easier for a kid and harder for an adult (remember when you refused to eat your vegetables). So, maintain your ability to say "no." You'll avoid wasting time doing things you don't want to do. That's not to say you shouldn't be open to trying new things—like vegetables. Rather, it's more about building up an indifference to peer pressure.

3. Always take hold of things by the smooth handle.

    Thomas Jefferson said that, and to me it means … don't make things more difficult than they need to be.

4. Write down your goals.

    As corny as it sounds … it helps to actually write your goals down. An article in *Forbes* talks about a Harvard study in which Harvard graduate students with written goals made twice as much money as their fellow students without written goals. I noticed the word "money" caught your attention. Well, actually it turns out the study is folklore. But c'mon, you don't need a study to prove to you that writing down your goals (and remembering to look at them) works. Every building ever built had a written plan describing what was needed to succeed. (Exception: that shed in the back of your grandfather's yard did not have a written plan.)

5. Do hard things.
   You're capable of doing big things. We all are. And doing big things is fun (and hard).

6. Make good friends and help them.
   Be the kind of friend you'd want someone to be to you. Entrepreneur James Altucher talks about treating people as though you secretly know today is their last day on earth. Treat everyone with kindness and consideration. Make them better because they know you.

7. Be kind and smile.
   Simple things you do can make the day better for you and everyone around you.

8. The world is a small place. The universe is a big place.
   You're now living in a world where much of the world is connected. And that can have far-reaching implications. Scientists estimate there's between 200 and 400 billion stars in our galaxy—the Milky Way.[13] And it's a normal-size galaxy. And there's between 100 and 200 billion galaxies in the universe. That calculates to (hmm, getting my calculator out) a 6 followed by 22 zeros. I don't even know what that means, but it's a big place. The good news is that your brain is the most complex thing known in the universe—and yippee … you've got one. It'll help you figure things out, and there's lots to learn.

9. Work hard.
   No matter what you do in life, going the extra mile (and likely then some) is the key to creating opportunities and moving you along the journey.

10. Work smart.
    This is the key to considering you're creating the right opportunities for your unique journey.

11. Learn every day.
    According to *Smithsonian Magazine*, there's about 37.2 trillion cells

in your body, and your body is constantly replacing old cells with new ones at the rate of millions per second.[14]   You get smarter and grow every year. When someone graduates from high school, they're a different person from when they started. Then, when they graduate from college, they're a different person from when they started college. And for those who don't go to college, they'll still grow and be a different person from all they learn in the working world. Even though learning is a natural thing for kids to do, believe it or not, it's easy for adults to stop learning. Don't stop learning. Learn so much that you become a better person every several years.

12. Don't compare yourself to others.
   There's over seven billion people in the world, but there's only one you.

13. Call home.

14. Don't believe in dogma.
   You'll hear a lot of things that probably don't make sense to you. That's your brain doing its thing. Proceed with a rational mind (even question things on this list).

15. Be blind toward race or color.
   This is so obvious from scientific and philosophical considerations that I don't even know what to write.

16. Don't be afraid to be embarrassed.
   Peer pressure can be hard to disregard. Everyone wants to be cool. Nobody wants to look bad. The best way to never be embarrassed is to never try anything that has a chance of failing. But that's an express train to the little town of mediocrity (kids, I know when you're rolling your eyes). If you study the greats, you'll see they all were focused on their dreams and had a healthy disregard for always wanting to look cool.

17. Believe in science (and don't forget love).
   This isn't to say science is always right, but it works dang well.

18. Follow the golden rule.
   Your grandmas were right … "Treat other people like you want to be treated."

19. Don't concern yourself with following the herd.

20. Work at being better every day.

21. Exercise.
We were made to move, and you should do so daily. Want proof? How many times have you heard lyrics playing through the house, "Tramps like us, baby we were born to run." Thank you, Bruce Springsteen.

22. Eat healthy.
Just one of the many, "Do as I say, not as I do."

23. Create more than you consume.
It's easy to consume too much content. It's not all bad (but most of it is). But remember to spend more time creating content than consuming. Creation is the act by which you learn and grow.

24. Participate more than cheer.
It's better to be out running in the rain by yourself, than cheering for a distant sports team playing on the television.

25. Remember to say, "Oh, wow."
Let yourself be awed by the day. Yes, I stole that lesson from my kids (love and adore you both, Dad).

Special note to the reader: Should you meet my kids, do not listen to their tales of how their dad doesn't do many of the above. Grown children are prone to great exaggeration.

What Running (Far) Has Taught Me About Work and Life

It was pitch dark, cold, and nearing 10 p.m. I came out of the woods after running 75 miles nonstop on the trail since starting earlier in the day. My body ached, but the worst part were the blisters on the soles of my feet. They were so deep that they were impossible to drain with a needle (believe me, I tried). Every step squished and hurt. Like. Hell.

I had 25 miles more to go.

My wife and kids were there, holding flashlights to see what was going on. I hobbled into a lawn chair. I changed my socks and shoes. I felt broken and beaten and pulled a towel over my head to kind of hide like an ostrich (truth is, along with my body being thrashed, my mind was fatigued, and for the first time since I was thirteen … I was starting to cry). My kids stood around me silently, wondering what I was going to do. I felt a hand on my shoulder, and that simple touch felt like being hard-wired to a source of energy and light.

We are bipedal creatures made to move. It helps us think and it helps us live. Whether walking around the block or running 100 miles, every person has his or her own reason for getting out the door and moving. The reasons include the fact that it's good for you. Often, it's the challenge of going beyond previous limits, pushing through a physical and mental challenge.

Running 100 miles isn't good for you. But neither is working awful hours week after week. But sometimes, going beyond what's normal gives us new perspectives and insights. It teaches us things we didn't know.

There's a lot about running (and sports in general) that's analogous to work and life. Pushing through seemingly intractable problems, balancing your resources, and learning how to keep yourself motivated.

Here are 17 lessons that running has taught me about work and life.

1. Break the work into stages.

    When you're lining up at the starting line, it's too intimidating to think about running 100 miles, or a marathon, or whatever your new barrier is. Work and life are the same way. If you're starting a new venture, developing a new product, or building a giant hovercraft—and you focus on all that's ahead, your reptilian brain will have you scurrying away in fear.

    While it's important to know the intended outcome ("We will launch the product in 100 days" or "I will finish this 100 miler"), at the same time, it's critical to break the effort into stages. If it's a product the team is working on, first there's a breadboard, or wireframes. Then there's a prototype or a minimum viable product (MVP) that can be used to begin improving and iterating. Whatever the big goal, it's mandatory to break it into achievable pieces, and move from successfully completing one and then the next. Basically, connecting the series of milestones that are necessary to succeed.

2. Fancy equipment isn't necessary.

    There are a lot of things that might be "nice" to have to help get the work done. But I don't think I've ever been involved in a project that had anywhere near everything we'd have liked. Use what you have, and move forward as best you can.

    Let me share a quick story … I was supporting a friend, Marshall Ulrich,[15] during what is considered to be the ultimate endurance run. Badwater is a 135-mile run (nonstop) through Death Valley during the hottest week of the year in July (typically 128 degrees F). He's a world-class runner and athlete, and his accomplishments are too long to begin mentioning here, but let me say, "He's the real deal."

    The night before the 135-mile run, we went out to the car to get his running shoes. Keep in mind, he's professionally sponsored. So, I figured we'd see a sizable inventory of new, state-of-the-art running shoes. Ulrich opens the trunk, and I see some climbing gear next to a spare tire. I ask, "Is this the climbing axe you used on Everest?"

    "Yea," he said, "that went to the top of the world with me" (side note, he'd also summited Mount Everest). Anyway, back to looking for the shoes. He's scrounging around with a flashlight and digs out a pair of running shoes so absolutely worn, dirty, and utterly dilapidated that I swear there was no pattern on the soles. You might wear them if you were painting a fence or roto-tilling the garden. He gave them a look and said, "These will do."

The lesson is—you don't need a perfect circumstance or perfect equipment to get started. Don't wait for the stars to align and for everything to be in place. Make a plan and get moving.

3. **Prepare by doing the work.**
You can't just show up and expect to create a world-changing product any more than you can show up and run for hours. But, with preparation and experience, anyone can do it. Really. As in sports and life, many people aren't willing to put in the time to become truly proficient in their craft. Do the work to prepare.

4. **Plan ahead.**
You know the importance of a plan. You also know that the plan will likely change (the real world has a way of doing that). Benjamin Franklin said, "If you fail to plan, you are planning to fail." I'm sure he knew what he was talking about—he's on the $100 bill.

5. **Attitude matters.**
Every worthwhile endeavor usually has a low point. In 100-mile ultramarathons, nights are usually the worst, as you've been running since six a.m. and sometimes you're just one negative thought away from throwing in the towel. Except that you're on a trail deep in the woods, and there's nobody to see you throw the towel.

On a few occasions while running ultramarathons, I've come across a body splayed out alongside the trail in the middle of the night. Here's what typically happens. First, you slow to a fast walk, so as not to step on any body parts. Then there's a five-second conversation that goes like this. I ask, "You ok?" The person on the ground responds, "Oh, yea. I'm good. I feel like I've been hit by a meteor, but I'll be moving again soon." Another saying among ultrarunners is "90 percent of the run is mental, and the rest is all in your head."

And that person lying in the dark? Surprisingly, you'll see him or her again with a finisher medal in hand. It's important to remember that sometimes a good attitude is all that keeps you in the game. Read the bios of innumerable disruptive luminaries, including Elon Musk, and you'll find it's a common occurrence. At one point they were struggling and saying, "I'll be moving again soon."

6. Expect the unexpected.
    Anticipate the problems along the way. Marketing specialist Guy Kawasaki in *The Art of the Start 2.0* suggests getting your business team together and having everyone list what possibly could go wrong that could derail your venture. Then go about making plans to eliminate those potential problems.

7. Be wary of small problems.
    We used to have a saying at one of the information technology professional services companies where I worked. "Panic early, panic often." It was a joke, but not really. The reality is that if you're aware of something that seems like it might be going sideways … address it immediately (or nearly so). Doesn't matter if it's a project falling behind, or chafing in a sensitive area. If you're aware of an issue, take care of it.

8. Manage your resources and progress.
    Running teaches you to be aware of your energy levels and your pace. The race director of the Umstead 100 Mile Endurance Run proffers some wisdom to all the runners the night before the run. "Drink before you're thirsty. Eat before you're hungry. Walk before you're tired." The same is true with your work and your life. Develop an awareness for how you're feeling. Slow down when you need to. Speed up when you can.

9. Be friendly and encouraging along the way.
    It doesn't matter if you're working on a rocket to Mars, developing a new software as a service (SaaS) offering or creating an animation classic; most everybody on the team is trying to make a go of it and succeed. It's all too easy to let the fatigue of the day drag you down. Resist. This doesn't mean you need to be an effervescent fountain of unjustified enthusiasm. But it does mean that part of your job is to always be professional and encouraging.

10. Manage what you can. Ignore the rest.
    We know this. Don't spend time and energy worrying about things you can't control.

11. Work with a team.

Markets are conquered, mountains are climbed, and championships are won by people collaborating together as a team. Even something as seemingly solo as running an ultramarathon depends on the support of others in the way of offering encouragement, aid station volunteers, a helpful crew, and someone to drive you home after the finish.

After finishing Badwater, the 135-mile run through Death Valley in July, David Goggins[16] a Navy SEAL, turned around and went back on the course to provide companionship and support to a straggling runner. That added at least another 30 miles to his effort. Even a solo endeavor like an ultramarathon presents an opportunity for truly unforgettable teamwork.

12. If it's not one thing, it's another.

Whether you're trying to move the needle on a project or you're trying to get out the door and moving, there will always be problems or challenges. That's why it's called work. Author Steven Pressfield calls this "Resistance."

13. It's harder than it looks.

Whether it's moving a business from A to B, raising a child, or running a marathon … No matter how much you talk to your friends who've done it or read books about it, it's actually harder that you expect. But here's the other truth, it's also more fun than you'd ever expect. And you'll learn more than you ever expected.

14. You can get through the worst of times.

At some point during the distance, you will likely have serious problems of one kind or another. You'll feel like the wheels are coming off, like you're beaten and finished. The important lesson is if you make adjustments and corrections, you will begin to feel better and get back on solid ground. It's worth remembering when things get really tough. Tough times don't last.

15. Don't quit, unless you have no choice.

While lecturing on the topic of ultrarunning, Ulrich was asked by a runner training for his first 100-mile run, "When would you quit? Like if you have blisters?" Marshall paused to think for a few seconds and then softly explained, "No, it would be like if you had a compound fracture." Ulrich once ran 200 miles with ice packs on his legs. Does that mean that Ulrich has never quit? Of course not, he's dropped out of races on rare occasion, and none of them involved a compound fracture. But it did involve him losing his positive attitude (reread number 5).

16. We're each an experiment of one.
    The great Dr. George Sheehan, a cardiologist, a runner, and the author of eight books, said, "We are each an experiment of one." What he meant is nobody can tell you exactly what's best for you. Or how to run your race or live your life.

17. The journey is the reward.
    Some miles will be glorious and some will be hell. But when you cross the finish line, your time really won't matter. The medal or industry awards won't matter. What will matter is the time spent moving forward. Living your life. Keep your head up, and look at the sights along the way. Encourage others. Smile as often as you can.

So, what happened to me after running 75 miles and sitting in the chair—broken, crying, and head covered with a towel? I sat for a minute, took every ounce of energy I could from that hand on my shoulder, slowly stood up, and told my family I loved them. And headed back into the dark, chasing the next 25.

Think Like an Immigrant

Here's a story with an ending I could have *never* seen coming. But I'll get to that once you hear the story.

It was 1915, and Diane Sabia was a young, 12-year-old girl when she left her home in Balvano, Italy, and crossed the Atlantic by ship to reach the United States. Diane carried her belongings in a cooking pot. She and her siblings were traveling with their mother, Antoinette Sabia, to reunite with their father who was waiting for them in America. Their father, Carmen Sabia, had gone ahead to work in America and establish some semblance of stability before his family followed from Italy.

As is typical of most dreams, establishing the footing in America had taken Carmen longer than anticipated. He had worked diligently since his arrival in the United States; yet it had been eight years since Carmen had seen his wife or his children.

As the ship approached the New York shore and Ellis Island came into sight, young Diane asked her mother, "How will you recognize papa after all the years?" Her mom smiled and said assuredly, "Don't worry, Diane, we'll recognize each other."

Reunited in the new land, they settled in Chicago, where Carmen continued working as a laborer in the railroad subway tunnels. The journey had taken several years, but finally they were all together in their new home—the United States.

There's a hunger to survive and thrive that is associated with immigrants. It's what allows them to arrive in a new land—often with next to nothing except their work ethic and a drive to create a better future. Pushing aside the fears of the unknown, they leave their native lands with heart-wrenching goodbyes to family and friends and head out into foreign territory. Many immigrants arrive with a minimal amount of currency. Many don't speak English. But they're brimming with optimism, hope for the future, and a profound drive to build. Their future and lives are at stake.

> *"Every aspect of the American economy has profited*
> *from the contributions of immigrants."*
> —John F. Kennedy

The success of immigrants is not anecdotal. Since the 1860s, immigrants to the United States have accounted for approximately 13 percent of the population. Yet, amazingly—40 percent of the Fortune 500 companies were started by immigrants or children of immigrants. When you're truly committed, few things can stand in the way of inexorable progress.

We can learn a lot from studying immigrants. They typically begin with little. Essentially no connections, zero financial resources, limited education, poor language skills, and significant cultural differences. Additionally, they often face prejudices and biases, which create an environment of further difficulty.

Yet, successful immigrants more than make up for these ostensible disadvantages with an abundance of tenacity and commitment to making forward progress. Immigrants bring an attitude of possibility, the belief that they can create something from nothing, and the burning desire to create a better life. And they often do.

Perhaps that's why in a *New York Times* article, titled "The Immigrant Advantage," the first line of the article began with the sentence, "If you want to die a successful American, especially in the heartland, it helps to be born abroad."[17]

Here are just some of the more than 200 Fortune 500 top American companies founded by immigrants or their children—Kraft, Ford, General Electric, Procter & Gamble, AT&T, Mattel, Google, McDonald's, Heinz, Home Depot, Hertz, Estée Lauder, UPS, Boeing, and Disney. A report, titled "The 'New American' Fortune 500" by the Partnership for a New American Economy, described these companies as "synonymous with America's leading role in the global marketplace."[18]

> *"There is no room in this country for hyphenated Americanism ... The*
> *one absolutely certain way of bringing this nation to ruin, of preventing*

*all possibility of its continuing to be a nation at all, would be
to permit it to become a tangle of squabbling nationalities."*
—Theodore Roosevelt

You would do well to think like an immigrant. The list of successful immigrants in the United States is basically limitless, but here are nine.

1. 1. Sergey Brin, Cofounder of Google
    Born in 1973, Brin immigrated with his parents to the United States from Russia when he was just six years old. While working on his doctorate at Stanford, he and his friend, Larry Page, built a Web search engine before starting Google in a garage. His net worth in 2018 is approximately $52 billion.

    *"Obviously everyone wants to be successful, but I want to be
    looked back on as being very innovative, very trusted and ethical
    and ultimately making a big difference in the world."*

2. Do Won Chang, Cofounder and CEO of Forever 21
    Do moved to the United States from Korea in 1984 and worked as a gas station attendant, a janitor, and also worked at a coffee shop. Three years later, he and his wife opened a clothing store. In 2018, Forever 21 does about $4 billion in annual sales, and the couple owns 100 percent.

3. Jerry Yang, Cofounder of Yahoo!
    At the age of ten, Yang immigrated from Taiwan with his mom and brother. Jerry knew just one English word—"shoe." He started Yahoo! in 1994. In 2018, he's an investor and advisor to several corporations, and is worth $2.7 billion.

4. Pierre Omidyar, Founder of eBay
    Omidyar is the son of Iranian immigrants, who were living in Paris when he was born. Shortly thereafter, they moved to the United States. Omidyar created a website called Auction Web that supported auctions. The service continued to evolve, eventually he renamed the company eBay and the rest is history.

*"Pursue your passion. If you're passionate about something
and you work hard, you will be successful."*

5. George Soros, Founder and Chairman of Soros Fund Management
   Soros was born in Hungary and had a difficult childhood, including a
   period where he lived in hiding to avoid the Nazi Germans occupying
   the country. He immigrated to England where he attended the London
   School of Economics and paid his way by working on the railroad
   and in local cafés. He immigrated to the US in 1956, and went on to
   become a wealthy businessman and philanthropist.

   *"Once we realize that imperfect understanding is the human condition,
   there is no shame in being wrong, only in failing to correct our mistakes."*

6. Andy Grove, Former Chairman and Former CEO of Intel Corporation
   Grove was born in Hungary, almost died from scarlet fever, and
   survived a Nazi occupation by taking on a false identity along with
   his mother, while his father was taken to a labor camp. They reunited
   after the war. Grove later escaped Hungary during the revolution
   in 1956 for Austria, and eventually made his way to the US the
   following year, where he was employed as a busboy. Grove graduated
   with a doctoral degree from UC Berkeley in 1963, and his career
   in technology led to his becoming the CEO of Intel. He wrote an
   excellent book, *High Output Management*, which I highly recommend.

   *"Success breeds complacency. Complacency
   breeds failure. Only the paranoid survive."*

7. Indra Nooyi, CEO of PepsiCo
   Indra was born in India and earned a master's degree there before
   coming to the US in 1978, where she earned a second master's degree
   at Yale. After a stint doing strategy consulting, she joined PepsiCo in
   1994, where she became CFO in 2001 and CEO in 2006. Since 2001,
   she has helped guide net profit from $2.7 billion to $6.5 billion, and
   has been recognized by *Time*, *Forbes*, and *Fortune* magazines.

"My mother's greatest gift was making me and my sister believe at a young age that we could achieve anything. While we were growing up in southern India, Mom always made certain we set our sights high and worked tirelessly to achieve our dreams."

8. Andrew Ly, Cofounder and CEO of Sugar Bowl Bakery
    Ly along with his family escaped Vietnam after the US departed the country. In 1978, they took a small boat, survived a harrowing eight-day-and-night journey at sea, which included being boarded by pirates who took everything but the clothes they were wearing. They began learning English when they arrived, worked hard, saved money, and bought a small coffee shop where they learned how to make doughnuts and muffins. In 2018, the bakery does over $1.8 million in annual sales.

    "When I came here, I didn't speak the language or have any money. I am proud that I've taken my family where they hesitated to go years ago. Whenever I mentor young people, I tell them, never give up. Work hard, have a good heart, and be disciplined. Those are the ingredients to success."

9. José Wilfredo Flores, Founder and President of W Concrete
    Flores came from El Salvador to escape the civil war when he was just 14. He made his way to Washington, DC, to live with his uncle and older brother. While he attended middle school, he worked part-time cleaning offices. At 15, he quit school, lied about his age using a fake ID and social security, and began working in construction. By age 25, he was supervising a crew of up to 50 people and was making $60,000. He eventually started W Concrete, which does several million dollars a year in sales.

    "In my country, there's no opportunity for poor people. The rich get richer and richer. The poor will always be poor and poor. Here, do it right and nobody can stop you."

And by the way, here's the part that I could have *never* seen coming about that 12-year-old, Italian, immigrant girl who carried her belongings in a cooking pot through Ellis Island on her way to meet her father, Carmen Sabia, whom she hadn't seen for eight years.

Although she never went to school beyond fifth grade, she was industrious and helped her parents with their family business. Eventually, she grew and married a young man who was also of Italian heritage, and they in turn had several children of their own. One of their boys grew and eventually married, and he in turn had a son ... and that was me (with the uncommon middle name of Carmen).

Thanks, Grandma, for being a brave little girl and coming home to a foreign land.

PART TWO

Invention and Innovation

Uncovering Hidden Solutions;
Creating New Value

Ten Myths of Innovation

There are a lot of myths about innovation. And not a single one involves chocolate. On the contrary, perhaps one of the most satisfying suggestions about being innovative is to have a chocolate bar in your pocket. There's concrete evidence that doing so had a huge impact on harnessing new technology into a product that had global impact. And we can thank American physicist Percy Spencer for the sweet lesson.

Percy was born in 1894 and had a difficult beginning as a child. When he was a baby, his father died, so his mother sent him to live with his aunt and uncle. Then when Percy was just seven, his uncle died. At the age of 12, Percy quit grammar school and began working 12-hour days in a local mill to support his aunt and himself. And that was the end of his formal education.

When he turned 18, Percy joined the Navy. While on night watch duty, he began reading whatever books he could find on the topic of wireless communications. He kept reading and taught himself calculus, chemistry, physics, and metallurgy.

After leaving the Navy, he went to work in 1939 for Raytheon. It was there, in 1945, that Percy and his chocolate bar made a discovery that changed the world. While he was working on a device called a magnetron, which generates short-wave radio waves, Percy noticed the chocolate bar in his pocket melted whenever he stood in front of the equipment. He had no idea what caused this, but soon discovered that it was due to microwaves. So he began modifying the equipment and, after several alterations, he built the first microwave oven.

So, chocolate is not only high in antioxidants and a cancer-fighting food, but it's also fundamental to technology commercialization. I like it even more. It certainly worked for Percy, who went on to receive 300 patents and numerous awards. All this was accomplished without a formal education, but with a curious mind, a desire to self-educate, and a chocolate bar.

So, take a bite of your chocolate bar and consider these myths about innovation.

1. Geniuses work alone.

   The world is full of solo inventors, but it's difficult to take technology to market by working alone in a basement or garage. Collaboration, teamwork, and feedback are often invaluable in creating something remarkable. Even if the initial idea originated from a visionary genius, having others contribute is essential to bringing a more evolved product to fruition. Marie Curie, Thomas Edison, and Alexander Graham Bell were all geniuses, and they worked alongside others.

2. Innovation happens somewhere else.

   For whatever reason, human nature often inclines people to think that great ideas or inventions happen "somewhere else." The reality is that inspiration for the idea—and the blood, sweat, and tears to bring the idea to life—can and does happen everywhere from A to Z. The Saturn V rocket was designed and built in Alabama, and the steamboat was invented in West Virginia.

3. Innovation happens in a flash of inspiration.

   Great ideas often happen in a flash, but execution doesn't. Albert Einstein wrote in his *Autobiographical Notes* that when he was 16 years old, he wondered what a light waveform would look like if he could observe a beam of light while traveling at the same speed. That thought experiment played a memorable role in his future and the development of the theory of relativity. While an idea or inspiration might come quickly, as it did for young Albert, the final solution (or product) typically takes significant effort and time to fully develop. The first wheels turned pottery in 3500 BCE and weren't used on chariots for three centuries. And monks were flying gliders a thousand years before the Wright Brothers' first flights.

4. Only large companies with vast resources can innovate.

   Actually, often it seems big companies are the least likely to innovate. Blockbuster Video could have come up with a better means of distributing DVDs (like startups Netflix and Redbox), but instead the company at its peak went from over 84,000 employees and 9,000 stores to bankruptcy. Or why didn't an internet company of Google's size and brainpower put several engineers on a project to create a text messaging-based platform like Twitter. Or consider the once dominant Kodak and its lack of innovation in digital cameras. The list of big companies that failed to innovate goes on and on.

5. **You need to be educated by a prestigious university.**
Percy Spencer did not have an auspicious beginning or a formal education—yet he was a great innovator. Benjamin Franklin was the son of a candlemaker and had only two years of formal schooling, but he was ambitious, worked hard, was resourceful, and was a great American inventor, scientist, and statesman. Ralph Lauren dropped out of college and never went to fashion school—yet his designs are considered iconic and his business savvy established him as one of the wealthiest people in America. Thomas Edison had three months of formal schooling, and attained over 1,500 patents and founded 14 companies, including General Electric. Steve Jobs, Mark Zuckerberg, and Bill Gates all dropped out of college. This by no means is an argument against education at a premier university, but rather a simple reminder that education can happen everywhere.

"What we have to learn to do, we learn by doing."
—Aristotle

6. **Your history indicates your future success.**
The world is full of countless examples of people who continued to invent and innovate, despite their earlier failures, until they succeeded. It's actually difficult to find successful innovators who didn't repeatedly fail.

7. **You can't "turn on" innovative thinking.**
Actually, to a large extent you *can* "turn on" creative thinking, and many people and organizations do exactly that. Bell Labs, Palo Alto Research Center, IDEO, Google, Nike, Apple and thousands more work at being creative and then work even harder to make ideas a reality.

8. **Set aside your emotions to innovate.**
Emotions are integral to humans and should be utilized in a manner

that assists with creativity. Emotions can be increased through music or movement or visual imagery (real or imagined). Find what works best for you, and bring a measure of emotion to your work.

9. A stimulating environment will stimulate thinking.
    Actually, wherever you can think freely and deeply is the best place to innovate. You don't need a pinball machine or a room full of beanbags nearby. Simply going for a walk or brainstorming with a few colleagues is sufficient inspiration. You might just need to be inspired. J. K. Rowling came up with the idea for Harry Potter while riding on a noisy, four-hour, train ride.

10. The best innovations are new creations.
    On the contrary, some of the greatest inventions ever are those that combine things that haven't been combined before. Combine a steam engine with steel wheels and you've created a locomotive train. Mix a telephone with a printer and you've got a fax machine. Marry a wireless communications system with a computer and you've got a smartphone.

So, take another bite of chocolate and get started!

A Billion Hours of Accidental Love

Albert Einstein supposedly said, "You can't blame gravity for falling in love." What he actually wrote (originally in German) was that "Falling in love is not at all the most stupid thing that people do—but gravitation cannot be held responsible for that."[19]

But Richard and Betty James certainly can blame gravity for their success.

It was 1943, and Richard was an engineer solving a problem for the US Navy. He was trying to isolate sensitive electronic equipment from the continual motion caused by rough seas. He thought the equipment could be suspended by springs.

He tried hundreds of different springs, and they cluttered his desk. At some point, one of the springs accidently slipped off his worktable, and fell onto the ship's deck where it landed on its end. It took a bounce, flipped onto its other end, and continued to move even farther away. Richard had work to do, and dropping things was annoying. But, at the same time, it was also funny to see that coiled spring saunter along.

He took it home to demonstrate it to his kids. His young son put it on top of the stairs and watched in amazement as the front of the coiled spring stretched to the step below, then began to seemingly walk itself down the stairs. His boy laughed hilariously. Soon other neighborhood kids were crowding around the stairs in his home.

Richard thought he might have a hit on his hand. He told his wife, Betty, "I think if I got the right property of steel and the right tension, I could make it walk!"

Richard kept his day job, and over the next couple of years their house filled with coiled springs of every conceivable dimension. He found a flat ribbon wire worked best, and settled on a ribbon 75 feet long, coiled 98 times.

They needed a name for their creation, and Betty searched the dictionary for inspiration. She came up with the word "slinky." That seemed to capture what the product did. They borrowed $500 and produced a quantity of 400 Slinkys.

People didn't seem to want it. One storekeeper said, "This is the atomic age. Kids want big, bright, fancy things with lots of color and lights. An old, beat-up spring!? We couldn't give that thing away. "

But the James persisted. At Christmastime, they talked Gimbels department store into letting them set up a ramp in the toy department to demonstrate the Slinky walking down the incline. They took 100 toys to the store and priced each one at $1.

Kids loved it. All 100 sold. Richard ran to get the remaining 300 units. Although these weren't even yet packaged, people were holding up their $1 bills and buying the Slinkys as fast as they could. Betty said later it was hard to find her husband in the crowd of kids. They sold out in 90 minutes. "We didn't sleep that night," they said.

Since that day, there've been over 350 million Slinkys sold. They now come in a variety of sizes. There are even multicolored Slinkys made from plastic, and, of course, the Slinky Dog, the dachshund from the animated film *Toy Story*.

Richard left the country in 1960 and joined a religious group in Bolivia. Betty ran the Slinky company as president from 1960 until 1998 when she sold the company for a "boatload of money." She died in 2008 at the age of 90.

Throughout her time, Betty always believed in keeping the price of the Slinky affordable. She wanted people to be able to afford the toy. She wanted kids to be able to play. "So many children can't have expensive toys, and I feel a real obligation to them. I'm appalled when I go Christmas shopping and $60 to $80 for a toy is nothing."

Everyone who's ever played with a Slinky has gravity to thank for causing that coiled spring to fall off Richard's desk and walk (down the steps) into our lives.

When Einstein remarked that gravity was not responsible for people falling in love—he was talking about falling in love with other people. But, gravity *is* responsible for people falling in love with Slinky.

Get a Slinky. Play with gravity. Fall in love.

Disastrous Problem + Resounding Failure = World-Changing Success

I t's a true story with multiple deaths caused mostly by a lack of experience. The story begins in one of the worst snowstorms to hit the Midwest.

Disastrous Problem

It was February 1934. The *Evening Independent* newspaper from Massillon, Ohio, ran the headline, "Worst Blizzard In Years Sweeps Northeastern Seaboard Region," and noted, "Snow ranging from six inches to one foot in depth blanketed New York City as the east suffered its worst winter weather in years."[20]

But all the young Army Air Corps pilot knew, while flying alone that day, was that he was trapped in a *complete whiteout*. After the navigational radio failed in his cockpit, and with zero visibility, he unknowingly had flown 50 miles off course. With few options, he made the decision to bail out of his plane into the biting, freezing wind. Immediately, his parachute became entangled on the plane he was trying to escape, and the young pilot was killed when his plane crashed outside a small Ohio town.

Later that same day, another Army Air Corps pilot was killed when he attempted a forced landing in Texas.

And the next day there was another Army Air Corps crash, which resulted in yet another death.

And it didn't end there. Within just a few weeks, there were more Army Air Corps plane crashes that resulted in the fatalities of 13 airmen.

The US Army Air Corps had undertaken all these flights with the simple purpose of delivering the US mail. The decision for the US Army Air Corps to carry the mail was made as a result of a congressional investigation, where it was learned that the mail routes, previously flown by large airlines, had been awarded in a manner that prevented smaller carriers from competing. So President Franklin D. Roosevelt's administration decided to have the US Army Air Corps fly the mail until the contracts could be fairly assigned.

But, the US Army Air Corps pilots were inexperienced with flying in inclement weather. In fact, their training did not provide the pilots with any means to accurately simulate the experience of flying in limited visibility, flying with failed electronic navigational equipment, or flying in bad weather. The result was the string of US Army Air Corps crashes and deaths, which famous aviator Eddie Rickenbacker publicly referred to as "legalized murder." [21]

The US Army Air Corps needed to find an immediate and effective solution.

Resounding Failure

Edwin Link was a young inventor with a shy demeanor, who really wanted to fly. In 1920, Link put down what was then the sizable sum of $50 for his first flying lesson. Here's what happened.

His flight instructor spent the time flying the plane doing loops and rolls and dives. It was thrilling and nauseating. It was also disappointing, as the pilot never let Edwin Link even touch the controls. Even as a student, Link realized it was not a good way to teach someone how to fly. And it was a realization that stuck.

Link's desire to fly remained, and over several years, he eventually got his pilot's license.

Edwin Link was a technician in his father's business—the Link Piano and Organ Company. He was also an avid tinkerer and inventor. While working there, Link cobbled together some steel piping and wiring used to assemble the organs and built the first airplane used for advertising. The plane utilized lights on the lower wing surfaces and was capable of spelling out messages— such as "Endicott-Johnson Shoes"—to anyone looking up.

But his quest to improve *how* pilots learned to fly remained with Link. In the 1920s, he fabricated a small cockpit and built controls that used pneumatics borrowed from his dad's organ factory to simulate the experience of flying. It was about the size of a desk and looked like a toy plane with short little stubby appendages for wings. Organ bellows would inflate or deflate, and cause the "plane" to bank, climb, or dive.

He called it the Link Trainer. When instruments began to be introduced, Link added them to his trainer, so pilots could practice using that equipment. Surely, he thought, the Link Trainer would transform the traditional (and expensive) way in which pilots were trained. He founded the Link Aeronautical Corporation in 1929 and pitched his invention to countless flight schools all across the country. None were interested. In fact, his only customers were amusement parks, which used the Link Trainer as a coin-operated carnival ride for kids.

World-Changing Success

Given the US Army Air Corps plane crashes and the airmen's deaths during the spring of 1934 when delivering mail, the brass needed to find a solution to their pilot's inexperience. Someone in the Air Corps had heard about the Link Trainer, and Edwin Link was asked to fly from his home in Cortland, New York, and provide a demonstration at the Newark airport, where the officials waited.

Only there was a problem. There was a rainstorm the day the Air Corps commanders requested Link to fly to Newark. Looking out into the thick fog at the airport, the officers made the decision to leave, because certainly nobody would be flying that day with zero visibility.

As they were departing, and with their backs to the runway, they heard the faint whine of an engine. Turning around, they watched Edwin Link emerge from the clouds just feet above the ground and touch down on the runway. Link had flown entirely "blind," using only the plane's instruments. After demonstrating the Link Trainer, the generals immediately ordered six units and the equipment was promptly put to use training Air Corps pilots.

Five years later, World War II began. In the following years, to meet the demands of training thousands of young pilots, over 10,000 Link Trainers were purchased. These trainers were credited with training more than half a million pilots.

Edwin Link invented one of the first electromechanical devices to simulate actual processes, and he revolutionized how training is done. His Link

Trainer was the forerunner for the flight simulators used by NASA for the Apollo missions and all other flight simulators used around the world today.

Edwin Link remained an innovator and inventor all his life. In addition to his pioneering contributions with flight simulators, Link was an avid marine scientist and ocean engineer. He went on to pioneer submersibles and undersea habitats. Link was curious, bold, stubborn, and scrappy.

Unlike Edwin Link's first flying lesson, where his instructor never let Link touch the controls, Link taught others by immediately putting the controls in the hands of the students. And he did so in a safe place (on the ground in a flight simulator), which allowed for repeated trial and error

What's more, Link didn't just teach people to fly. Link taught the world *how to learn* how to fly.

Advice for Your Journey

❝ Hi, Steve," I said, while shaking his hand. "Thanks for all the work and all the great products." He looked at me, smiled slightly, and nodded.

There are a few things I know for certain about life. Here is one of them. You come into the world a helpless naked baby, and you leave the world and take nothing with you. Hopefully, the middle is filled with many years of living a full life and making a positive difference. A beginning, an end, and "let's see what the heck you can do in the middle."

There are probably a few more things I know with certainty, like I love my family, and chocolate mousse is delicious, but no more come to mind. Call me "master of the obvious."

Singer/songwriter Kevin Welch summarized it fairly well, "There will be two dates on your tombstone and all your friends will read them. But all that is going to matter is that little dash between them."

The dash is where it's at, and if you're like me, you probably want to live a great dash. Certainly it will have its share of ups and downs. Great work and bad work. Great bosses and bad bosses. Some amazing experiences and some bad experiences. All in all, it will make an interesting journey. Maybe even a hero's journey.

The Hero's Journey was introduced by Joseph Campbell, an American author and lecturer, who'd written a number of books on mythology, including *The Hero with a Thousand Faces* and *The Power of Myth*. Campbell summarized the hero's journey like this.

"A hero ventures forth from the world of common day into a region of supernatural wonder: fabulous forces are there encountered and

> *a decisive victory is won: the hero comes back from this mysterious*
> *adventure with the power to bestow boons on his fellow man."[22]*

That storyline should sound familiar. George Lucas' Star Wars saga was heavily influenced by the book. As was *The Lion King, The Hobbit, The Wonderful Wizard of Oz, The Matrix*, and countless other stories.

Which brings me to Steve Jobs and the dash between his years, which was a hero's journey.

In 1995, Steve was interviewed at length by Robert Cringely, a journalist and former Apple employee. At the time, Steve was CEO of NeXT computer and software company and Pixar. It was 18 months before he'd return to Apple, and two years before he'd take over as Apple CEO. After taping the interview, the master tape was sent overseas and went missing. A VHS copy was found after Jobs died, and the film was released in 2012 in its entirety as *Steve Jobs: The Lost Interview.*[23]

You can learn a tremendous amount by watching the interview, and I would urge you to do so.

In the movie, Steve candidly discusses his thoughts and experiences. His sincerity is palpable. His answers are full of insights and advice. Looking back, we know that Steve was somewhere in the middle of his hero's journey. You are likely somewhere in the middle of yours. His thoughts and advice are sure to be helpful in your quest.

1. On focus and money.

> *"It's interesting. I was worth over a million dollars when I was 23, and over $10 million when I was 24, and over $100 million when I was 25. And, it wasn't that important. Because I never did it for the money."*

It's easy to chase the wrong thing. To get transfixed on a shiny object (money, title, whatever) and lose sight of what you really want your life to be about. Not that money isn't important. But relatively speaking, not so much.

Steve went on to say, "The most important thing was the company, the people, the product we were making. What we were going to enable people to do with these products."

Good advice. Focus on the people and the work.

2. Be enthusiastic (even if it blinds you).

It's sometimes good to be obsessive (I hope my family reads this). Steve was known for being extremely enthusiastic about new products that he thought could and should change the world. He talked about visiting Xerox PARC (later Palo Alto Research Center), and how he missed two of the three revolutionary things he was shown, because he was so enamored with the first thing that fired his imagination.

"They showed me really three things. But I was so blinded by the first one that I didn't even really see the other two. One of the things they showed me was object oriented programming. They showed me that, but I didn't even see that. The other one they showed me, really a network computer system. I didn't even see that.

I was so blinded by the first thing they showed me, which was the graphical user interface. I thought it was the best thing I'd ever seen in my life. And within you know, ten minutes, it was obvious to me that all computers would work like this someday."

3. Getting through the inevitable roadblocks.
   I've had my share of obstacles, problems and challenges. Want proof that everyone has his or her share? Here's how Steve described his team's embrace of the computer mouse.

   "Well, I got our best people together and started working on this... and they didn't get this idea. They didn't get it. I remember having dramatic arguments with some of these people. I remember arguing with these folks, people screaming at me that it would take us five years to engineer a mouse and cost $300 to build. And I finally got fed up and just went outside and found David Kelly design, and asked him to design me a mouse, and in 90 days we had a mouse that we could build for 15 bucks that was phenomenally reliable."

4. Process versus product.
   The interviewer suggests to Steve that perhaps there's a dark side to corporations. Steve responds by explaining the difference between doing things efficiently and doing the right thing.

   "It's that people get confused. Companies get confused. When they start getting bigger, they want to replicate their initial success. And a lot of

them think, 'Well, somehow there's some magic of how that success was
created.' So they start to institutionalize process across the company.
And before long, people get confused that the process is the content.
In my career, I've found that the best people are the ones that really
understand the content. And they're a pain in the butt to manage. But
you know, you put up with it, because they're so great at the content.
That's what makes great products. It's not process, it's content."

5. On the reality of the grind.
    After a long thoughtful pause, Steve talks about *how* great products are
    made. A wonderful answer, forged in the real world of sweating and
    arguing the details, and pushing the product toward what's possible.
    The first sentence alone is worth the price of admission, and embodies
    his ethos for bringing a great product to market.

"There's a tremendous amount of craftsmanship in between a great idea
and a great product. And as you evolve that great idea, it changes and
grows. It never comes out like it starts because you learn a lot more as
you get into the subtleties of it. And you also find there are tremendous
trade-offs that you have to make. I mean you know there are just
certain things you can't make electrons do, there are certain things you
can't make plastic do, or glass or factories do, or robots do. And as you
get into all these things, designing a product is keeping five thousand
things in your brain, these concepts, and fitting them all together
and continually to push to fit them together in new and different
ways to get what you want. And every day you discover something
new that is a new problem or a new opportunity to fit these things
together a little differently. And it's that process ... that is the magic."

6. A metaphor for team interaction (and friction) in making a great
    product.
    Metaphors, or stories, can become the framework for our
    understanding. Steve describes an experience he had as a kid and
    uses it as a metaphor for moving from a prototype to a beautiful
    finished quality product. It's an analogy that resonated with me, as I
    experienced the exact same thing after receiving a rock tumbler for
    Christmas as a little kid. After weeks (in my case) of polishing, it was
    the same wide-eyed amazing results.

This might be the best description I've ever heard as to why it's imperative to actively engage as a team throughout the development process.

〜〜〜〜〜〜〜〜〜〜〜〜〜

"When I was a young kid, there was a widowed man that lived up the street. And he was in his 80s; he was a little scary looking. And I got to know him a little bit. I think he might have asked me to mow his lawn or something. And one day he said, 'Come on into my garage, I want to show you something.' And he pulled out this dusty old rock tumbler. It was a motor and a coffee can and a little band between them. And he said, 'Come on with me.' And we went out to the back and we got some rocks. Just some regular, old, ugly rocks.

And we put them in the can, with a little bit of liquid, and a little bit of grit powder. And we closed the can up. And he turned the motor on, and said, 'Come back tomorrow.' And this can was making, you know, a racket as the stones went around.

And I came back the next day, and we opened the can and we took out these amazingly beautiful polished rocks. The same common stones that had gone in, through rubbing against each other like this, creating a little bit of friction, creating a little bit of noise, had come out these beautiful polished rocks.

And that's always been in my mind, my metaphor for a team working really hard on something they're passionate about. That it's through the team, through that group of incredibly talented people, bumping up against each other, having arguments, having fights sometimes, making some noise, and working together, they polish each other and they polish the ideas. And what comes out are these really beautiful stones."

〜〜〜〜〜〜〜〜〜〜〜〜〜

7. On hiring the best people.

〜〜〜〜〜〜〜〜〜〜〜〜〜

"Most things in life, the dynamic range between average and the best is at most two to one. Right, like if you go to New York City, and you get an average taxi cab driver versus the best taxi cab driver, you're probably going to get to your destination with the best taxi

cab driver like maybe 30 percent faster. You know, an automobile— what's the difference between average and the best? Maybe, I don't know, 20 percent? The best CD player and an average CD player? I don't know, 20 percent? So two to one is a big, big dynamic range in most of life. In software, and it used to be the case in hardware too, the difference between average and the best is fifty to one. Maybe one hundred to one. Ok. Very few things in life are like this. But what I was lucky enough to spend my life in, is like this. And so, I've built a lot of my success off finding these truly gifted people and not settling for B and C players, but really going for the A player."

8. On being direct.
    Steve could be brutally blunt, demanding, and hard to please. Although perhaps an innate characteristic, he describes his thinking underlying his approach.

    "The most important thing I think you can do for someone who is really good and is being counted on, is to point out to them when their work isn't good enough. And to do it clearly and to articulate why and to get them back on track. And you need to do that in a way that does not call into question your confidence in their abilities, but leaves not too much room for interpretation that the work they've done for this particular thing is not good enough to support the goal of the team. And that's a hard thing to do. And I've always taken a direct approach."

9. On being wrong.
    Steve could be stubborn and insistent. Yet would change his mind if presented with a convincing argument otherwise. As an example, years later Steve was adamant that Apple wouldn't sell apps from third parties, until he was eventually convinced otherwise.

    "I don't care about being right. I just care about success. So, you'll find a lot of people who will tell you I've had a strong opinion and they've presented evidence to the contrary, and five minutes later I've completely changed my mind... And I'll admit that I'm wrong a lot. It doesn't matter to me too much. What matters to me is that we do the right thing."

10. His evident passion for product aesthetic and culture.

When the conversation turns to Microsoft, it's fascinating to hear Steve articulate his fully formed ethos that a product be more than merely useful. That a product should be a work of craftsmanship, art, and subtlety—while providing real value to the user.

> *"I have a problem with the fact that they [Microsoft] just make really third-rate products. Their products have no spirit to them. Their products have no kind of spirit of enlightenment about them. They are pedestrian. And the sad part is most customers don't have a lot of that spirit either. But the way that we're going to ratchet up our species is to take the best and to spread it around to everybody, so that everybody grows up with better things. And starts to understand the subtlety of these better things."*

11. Why Steve Jobs was relentless.

> *"That of all the inventions of humans, the computer is going to rank near, if not at, the top as history unfolds and we look back. And it is the most awesome tool that we have ever invented. And I feel incredibly lucky to be at exactly the right place in Silicon Valley, at exactly the right time historically, where this invention has taken form. And, as you know, when you set a vector off in space, if you can change its direction a little bit at the beginning it gets dramatic when it gets a few miles out in space. I feel that we are still really at the beginning of that vector, and if we can nudge it in the right directions, it will be a much better thing as it progresses on."*

That was some of the thinking that led to a brilliant dash between the year of Steve's birth and death. The dash that was truly a hero's journey of mythical proportion.

I'm going to take those lessons, combine them with my experiences, and add them to my dash.

My sincerest hope is that you do too. And maybe someone will come up to you and shake your hand, and say, "Thanks for all the great work and all the great products." And you'll smile slightly and nod.

How a Doctor Killed My Idea, and I Stopped the Madness

My son sent me a text from college. Usually he texts me to give me some news, like about his new part-time job at FedEx. Or how cold it is in the Northeast. Smart kid. He doesn't text me about money. When he needs money, he reaches out to his mom. He knows I wouldn't have a clue how to log-in and transfer moola to his account. At least I think that's how it works. I honestly don't know.

He texted me to ask if his friend could call me, "to talk about his invention."

"Of course," I immediately replied.

Later that evening, a college student named Eric called. And in a youthful voice filled with hope and an enviable amount of enthusiasm—proceeded to breathlessly summarize his idea. At this point, it was really just a concept. He had made no mockups or prototypes. He hadn't done napkin sketches or basic research on the internet to see if a similar product already existed.

Yet, I *loved it*! And by "it," I mean the entire conversation—his enthusiasm, hope, uncertainty, and questions as to what to do next. There was something viscerally wonderful about listening to his enthusiasm of a new idea. I loved it all.

I pictured a kid carefully holding an egg, while excitedly pointing out a little beak just starting to break through. I needed a reminder of that unmitigated enthusiasm.

In the early 1970s, when I was about 15 years old, I had an idea for a shoe insert. I imagined it would be like a little bladder or pillow you'd insert into your shoe. Only special. There were shoe inserts at the time, but they were made from hard plastic or foam. My idea was to have an insert filled with either water or gel. Something that would be like "walking on water." That's how I imagined it. It seemed like a darn good idea to me.

My dad told me to walk into town and introduce myself to the podiatrist. That's exactly what I did. I don't remember the podiatrist's name. But I clearly remember his office and what he looked like. He was old. When you're 15, everybody over 30 looks old. But this doctor was old-old.

The meeting lasted about two minutes. No exaggeration. Maybe less. I explained my idea to him, describing enthusiastically the benefits of walking on little waterbeds for your feet. The doctor wore glasses. I remember thinking that he'd probably seen thousands of feet. I stared at his face. He showed no interest or enthusiasm. He never nodded and his eyes never widened.

He slowly turned to his right, and pointed with his hand at a chest-high bookshelf on the wall behind him. The shelf was nearly the entire width of the wall and was lined with books. They all had the same dark-green leather cover, like an encyclopedia. He turned back to me.

"Do you know, the feet and hands have more than half of the bones in your entire body?" he asked.

"Wow! I didn't know," I replied politely.

He continued. "Oh, yes. The foot is complicated, really complicated. And it has been studied extensively. Everything about the foot is known. There have been many books written about just the foot." He motioned again to the books on the shelf. "All those books are just about the foot."

"Wow," I said again.

"Oh, yes. Everything has already been done," he said.

I walked the mile back home.

"How'd it go?" my dad asked.

"Well," I shrugged, "the doctor said everything is known about the foot. And he didn't seem to like my idea too much."

And that was it. I basically never thought about my waterbed insert foot idea again. Well, at least for the decade or so until *all the different companies* started coming out with gel inserts and soles.

Here's what I told the college student Eric.

1. That might well be an *awesome* idea!
   Know this fact. Nobody can really tell you if an idea is a "good" idea
   or a "bad" idea, for the simple reason that *nobody really* knows. Every
   failed company has had its share of believers, just as every grand-
   slam company—from Google to Twitter to Apple—had its share of
   knowledgeable people who judged its success unlikely. This isn't to say
   that asking for someone's thoughts, opinion, or advice is a bad idea.
   But it is a bad idea to take any one person's opinion as a clairvoyant
   view into the future or as a meaningful judgment about the idea.

2. It's really about the execution (not the idea).
   Somewhat counterintuitively, it's not so much about having a *great*
   idea. Ideas are everywhere. And everybody has them. What actually
   does matter, is *doing* something with the idea. And, of course, doing
   it in a unique manner. Mrs. Fields didn't invent the chocolate chip
   cookie. Starbucks former CEO Howard Schultz wasn't the first person
   to sell coffee.

3. There is *no* downside to pursuit.
   Go after this idea. Learn more about the market. What currently
   exists that's similar? What does the market say about the need?
   Everything you learn and experience will put you well on the way
   to better understanding *how* market research, product development,
   prototyping, boot-strapping/fundraising, and business actually work.
       Get on the internet and query what customers are saying about
   this need. Go to a local hobby store and buy some material and start
   experimenting at home.
       Collect data. Make some charts and graphs of your experiments.
   Learn the basic math or engineering related to the invention.
       Make a quick prototype. Show it to friends … or better yet potential
   customers, and get their feedback.
       Ask your professors for help and advice.
       Any one of those things is better than watching television or
   hanging out. And being a bit atypical, because you're working on
   something and skipping some typical social activities, will be good
   experience.

4. Prepare yourself to answer questions.
   Anticipate the questions you'll be asked about your idea. Determine

if you should seek a partner or investor. Be able to articulate the problem. Be prepared to discuss what already exists on the market. Explain in 30 seconds how your idea is an improvement. Show some basic market research. Show some test results. Put together some rough pricing estimates.

5. Use this idea as an opportunity to develop yourself.
   Everything you experience and learn by exploring and trying to bring this product idea to fruition will not only make you a better student and give you better insights into business, but it will make you better at life. That's a far-reaching statement, but I believe it's absolutely true.

6. Everything you do and learn, contributes to what you know and who you are. And there is *no better* way to learn than by doing. No textbook, no story, no friend, no teacher can take the place of learning by doing.

"Self-education is, I firmly believe, the only kind of education there is."
—Isaac Asimov

And, Eric, one thing I can promise you. Regardless of where this idea leads. You will absolutely be a better person for pursuing this idea.

I imagine it'll be a fun experience, like walking on little waterbeds.

Frozen Fish Inspired an Innovation Revolution

There's no way anyone could have predicted that a frozen fish would inspire someone to pursue an invention of such significance—that it would not only create an entirely new industry and change the world, but would also have you eating your vegetables. But that's what happened as a direct result of a curious American inventor.

His name was Clarence, and he was born in Brooklyn in 1886. Clarence attended Amherst College for two years prior to leaving school due to financial difficulties. He then went to work for the US Agriculture Department, where he became an assistant naturalist and was assigned to work in the western United States. In 1912, he was assigned to the far northeast region of Canada. It was there that the Inuit taught Clarence how to ice fish and how to freeze the day's catch. And that's when Clarence had his epiphany.

The Challenge of Seeing the Curve Ahead

Technology entrepreneur, writer, and venture capitalist Guy Kawasaki has talked for decades about the challenges inherent in anticipating change and the even greater challenge of then getting ahead of the change, of seeing what everyone else is missing. Basically, it rarely happens. Though, in hindsight—the upcoming disruption should've been obvious. There are countless stories about smart people focusing on the work at hand and missing the change ahead.

Here's one that involves ice.

In the early 1800s, there was a huge business in the northeastern United States related to harvesting ice. Men would venture out onto a frozen lake, cutting huge blocks of ice chunks, and loading them onto horse-drawn carts, where they were then taken and put into storage. Later they would be delivered to "iceboxes." There were dozens of companies in this business, employing many people harvesting and transporting the ice.

All that was upended once commercial refrigeration was possible beginning about 1850. Once that technology existed, water could be frozen into ice wherever the refrigeration equipment was located. And, of course, eventually these facilities were located everywhere and were no longer dependent on a cold winter to produce ice. And then, in the 1920s, the home refrigerator was introduced, and that upended the commercial refrigeration businesses.

Here's what's interesting. None of the companies harvesting ice from the lakes made the transition to the commercial refrigeration industry. And decades later, none of the commercial refrigeration companies transitioned to the home refrigeration market. Oftentimes, it's the people outside the industry, those unencumbered from the accepted thinking, who drive the next disruption cycle.

Back to Clarence

Clarence was not in the refrigeration business. But during his time in northeast Canada, Clarence learned how the Inuit rapidly would freeze their catch, and he couldn't help but notice how incredibly fresh the fish tasted once thawed. It was something he recognized as superior to the frozen, mushy, and dry fish he'd eaten everywhere else.

The concept stuck with him, and, in 1922, Clarence Birdseye began experimenting. He had little money, so with meager funds and in an attempt to replicate the conditions he experienced in northeastern Canada, he bought ice, an electric fan (to create wind chill), and salt (to lower the freezing point).

He learned that conventional freezing methods of the day were far slower in comparison to how the Inuit froze their fish. He observed through a microscope that the conventional freezing methods resulted in much larger ice crystals, and that the large crystals damaged the fish tissue when thawing—hence the mushy taste typical of slowly frozen fish.

He started a company called Birdseye Seafoods Inc. to commercialize his discovery—but the company went bankrupt a couple of years later, as there was little demand from a slow-to-adopt market.

Clarence Birdseye kept working, and developed an entirely new way to quickly freeze packaged fish by squeezing the packages between two frozen belts under pressure. He patented his idea, secured backing from three wealthy partners, formed a new company called General Seafood Corporation, and returned to the fast-freeze fish business. This time, the market was ready—and within a few years, he expanded beyond freezing fish to fast-freezing chicken, fruits, and vegetables.

Clarence went on to develop refrigerated display cases for grocery stores. He leased refrigerated boxcars to transport the frozen foods by rail. In the end, Clarence Birdseye created what became the frozen foods industry. He held nearly 300 US and foreign patents in his lifetime and was inducted into the National Inventors Hall of Fame in 2005.

The brand Birds Eye remains a household name. And it all started when a curious man met a frozen fish.

Twenty of the Greatest Inventions of All Time

I was flat on my back. Everybody standing around me had their faces covered. They covered my mouth and nose with a rubber mask; told me to close my eyes and start counting backward from 10—which is exactly what I did. I tried to be brave, but it was scary. 10 … 9 … 8 … Maybe I got to 5 or 4. And then I passed out. I was seven years old and in the hospital to get my tonsils removed.

That's a roundabout way of explaining why anesthesia is on my list of "20 of the Greatest Inventions of All Time." That was a sufficiently memorable experience. Though if there was any doubt, there have been a few subsequent visits to the dentist that further solidified my thinking.

Although not as subjective as listing the top 20 movies of all time, listing 20 of the greatest inventions is nonetheless open to discussion and argument. Our personal experiences and the era in which we live influence what we rank as important. Also, an invention's impact might not be apparent for decades, so we need the perspective of time to understand an invention's utility and reach. Time is clearly necessary for the impact of an invention to shake out.

My logic of what makes this list is primarily based on what has most benefitted humankind. Again, it's difficult to compare some of these inventions, or to determine exactly where they rank. Both the airplane and the computer are in my top twenty, but there wasn't a fancy algorithm used to order them, or even that put them on the list in the first place. It was just a matter of my estimation.

As a side note, I thought about listing "The Lever" or even "The Sewing Needle," as those were also important and fundamental "tools," but in the end decided not to include them as "inventions," because levers and needles exist in nature (sticks and thorns) and somebody just had to start using them.

As a second side note, there were some profound ideas that I thought might be considered great inventions—such as the "The Scientific Method" or "Evolutionary Biology" or theories of the universe, but I also decided those would better be classified as "ideas," because they exist without a specific invented product.

Here then is my list of "20 of the Greatest Inventions of All Time," along with a brief explanation as to why.

1. 1. The Wheel

    The wheel is everywhere, but interestingly historians say the first wheels were not used for transportation. Evidence shows that the first wheels were potter's wheels that were created about 3500 BCE in Mesopotamia. They were used for chariots about 300 years later.

2. The Printing Press

    Before Johannes Gutenberg invented the printing press and movable type in the early 1400s, books or other documents were generated by hand. Once the printing press mechanized book making, the number of books grew exponentially to 20 million volumes by 1500, and then upward of 200 million just 10 years later. This explosion of books drove literacy and the spread of knowledge around the globe.

3. The Plow

    The plow allowed soil to be more easily turned, so the nutrients buried several inches underground would be brought closer to the surface, while at the same time burying the grass and vegetation, which would decompose and provide more nutrients to whatever crops were planted. When pulled by an animal, a plow greatly improved food production.

4. Cement

    The invention of cement allowed for everything from pottery, housing, and canals. It's been described as the bond that held civilization together.

5. The Steam Engine
   The steam engine was the dawn of the industrial age. Invented by James Watt in 1781, the steam engine was initially a relatively small, 10-horsepower engine, that within a dozen years grew a thousandfold to 10,000 horsepower. That is basically the doubling of horsepower every year (I just did it on a napkin), and that's Moore's law.

6. Penicillin
   One of the first drugs to be used against disease, penicillin has improved and saved countless lives. Although penicillin was discovered by Scottish scientist and Nobel Prize laureate Alexander Fleming in 1928, it proved difficult to produce in quantities until the mid-1940s. In fact, the first patient was treated with US-made penicillin from Merck in 1942, and that single patient used half the total supply produced. Eventually, the production process was sorted out, and the US produced 646 billion units per year in 1945.

7. The Light Bulb
   On the back of my business card is a quote from Thomas Edison. "Results! Why, man, I have gotten a lot of results! I know several thousand things that won't work." I'm actually reading it now, and it's after midnight (and dark outside).

8. The Lens
   The invention of an optical lens allowed the unseen to be seen, and therefore the unknown to be known. What was previously invisible to the naked eye—whether microscopic organisms or distant stars—all were made visible by the invention of the lens.

9. Paper
   Paper and the printing press worked hand-in-hand to drive literacy, spread knowledge, and improve the world.

10. Vaccines
    Receiving a vaccine is basically a way of getting the body to fight and then remember a disease. Then when it is encountered in the future, the body is prepared to recognize and destroy the disease before it can multiply in large numbers. The World Health Organization reports (in 2018) that licensed vaccines are currently available for 26 diseases with another 24 in the pipeline.

11. The Computer

The small amount of programming I did was in high school and then in engineering school at college. Like most everyone at the time, we held our punch cards together with rubber bands and spent hours waiting for the ream of green and white printout. A missing comma or extra period somewhere in our punch cards would result in an error message, and we'd have to make the correction and then start all over. It was painful. There was only one building on campus where our programs were run—and it was in the basement of the math and science building. For some reason, we were always there late at night, and it always smelled like peanut butter and sweat. We'd hand our rubber-banded stack of punch cards though a window to an operator, and he went into a back room and handed them over to HAL from *2001: A Space Odyssey.*

It was incredible to see the emergence of the personal computer. One of my engineering friends built a computer in his dorm room in the late 1970s. I remember several years later being fascinated watching a plotter generate a graph, or the first time I used a graphical user interface with a mouse.

Like many of you, since then I've used a computer nearly continuously throughout my career. My amazement continues to grow, along with the increased performance and capabilities. It's "a bicycle for our minds," as described by Steve Jobs.[24]

12. The Telephone

As with many inventions, the telephone was developed by several different people who each made contributions. The telephone made voice communications possible, and that resulted in lessening the distance between people. It also lets you talk to your mom when you're far away, and say "love ya, Mom."

13. The Internet and the World Wide Web

The internet provides untold utility to billions of people around the world. Anyone (anywhere) with a basic computer and internet access has access to a treasure trove of essentially unlimited information. Even more mind-boggling, it provides anyone (anywhere) with a communications platform with greater capability and greater reach than what the most powerful commercial broadcasting companies had even 10 years ago. It's like giving you the keys to a worldwide media empire. Its impact is still nearly unimagined.

14. The Automobile

One of the first complex machines to be mass-produced, the automobile quickly became ubiquitous and necessary. It drove the construction of highways and byways, affected where people worked and lived, and profoundly affected the social fabric of America.

15. The Flush Toilet

Nick Veléry wrote an article for *The Economist* where he described the flush toilet as more miraculous than the invention of antibiotics. "Without plumbed sanitation within the home to dispose of human waste, we would still be living in a brutal age of cholera, dysentery, typhus and typhoid fever—to say nothing of bubonic plague."[25]

Not surprisingly, the earliest history of a toilet that used water as a means of flushing, used the flow of river water diverted through a drainage system to carry waste downstream. Probably the phrase "location, location, location." was heard shortly thereafter.

16. Anesthesia

Hard to believe, but anesthesia was invented only in the mid-1800s. I'm not sure what was used before the invention of anesthesia, but I would hate to have had a major injury that required a trip to the surgeon or dentist before that time.

17. The Airplane

If you have the chance, you should visit Kill Devil Hills in North Carolina. That's where, in 1903, the Wright brothers first flew a controlled, heavier-than-air, powered flight. Out among the grassy sand fields, the distances of their first few flights are shown with markers. There's a model of the Wright Flyer and of their modest cabins where they lived and worked during their visits from Ohio to North Carolina, where they made repeated attempts to fly. It's hallowed ground.

It's hard to believe that just a little more than 50 years later, Boeing introduced the 707. And just 66 years after the Wright brothers first flew, in 1969, *Apollo 11* landed on the Moon. Hallowed ground indeed.

18. Semiconductors

Made mostly from silicon, the second most abundant element in Earth's crust, semiconductors are the foundation of our computers (now in our cars, homes, phones, and on our wrists) and currently a $330-billion global business.

19. The Radio

Guglielmo Marconi patented the radio a few years before 1900, but it wasn't until the 1920s that it worked well enough to be used as a medium for news and entertainment. Although the telegraph allowed for immediate communications over long distances, the radio provided the ability to effectively communicate with huge numbers of people directly by voice.

20. Genetics

People have been studying, experimenting, and manipulating plants and animals since ancient times through selective pairing, but Gregor Mendel is considered a leader of modern genetics. In the mid-19th century, he studied the nature of inheritance in plants.

Bonus 21. Steelmaking

Learning how to create quality steel in large production quantities provided the material for the industrial age. It is a fundamental component within virtually every industry—automobile, aircraft, construction, machinery, ship building, and manufacturing.

Bonus 22. The Telegraph

The telegraph actually had a long process of improvements, one could argue with the beginning of smoke signals and reflected light, through electrical telegraphs like that used to tap out and send Morse code, and continuing on through wireless telegraphy.

As with most such "top lists," there's subjectivity. Your own list will not be exactly like mine. Actually, my own list might change the next time I give it a look. Even luminaries disagree.

In 2013, *The Atlantic* surveyed a dozen incredibly smart leaders within technology, science, and engineering and asked them to list the inventions that had the greatest impact on civilization. The editors compiled and weighted the lists submitted by everyone, and then published "The 50 Greatest Breakthroughs Since the Wheel."[26] I didn't see the individual lists, but I do know this. If they were seven years old and getting their tonsils out, they'd put anesthesia (very) near the top.

Moving the Bullseye

People were dying from their bad hearts. So doctors used a device to help save their lives. But, there were problems with the device, and improvements needed to be made. Maybe the solution to making the device better will be immediately apparent to you. Like most things, the answer is simple once you see it. Though honestly, even if I hadn't been shown the simple solution, I'm not sure that it would have been apparent to me.

Throughout my career, I've been lucky to work with some really smart people. The two key people related to this innovation were John Lucas and Robert Schock. Bob has a doctoral degree in engineering, and I call him "the professor." It just seems to fit. There were other people involved, of course, but these two wizards led the effort.

There were a lot of limitations, physical restrictions, on what could be done. As it turned out, the problem was solved by thinking about it from an entirely new perspective. But, I'm getting ahead of myself.

Let me give you a little background and show you an illustration. Then you can solve the problem, perhaps just by thinking about it, or maybe scribbling a bit on a napkin. In any event, you won't need a calculator or even math.

As mentioned at the outset, people were dying. In fact, every year, thousands and thousands of people went to hospitals with a weak or damaged heart. These weak hearts weren't able to pump sufficient amounts of blood through the bodies of these folks. Not good.

To help these troubled hearts, doctors sometimes insert an intra-aortic balloon (IAB) to help the heart pump blood through the body. An IAB is actually simple to describe. Think of it like a tube (called a catheter) that's about a meter in length (and about twice the diameter of an iPhone charging cord). At the front end, there's a hot dog-size balloon. If you looked at a cross section of the catheter, you'd see it's actually a tube inside another tube. The inside tube is used to insert a metal wire that guides the catheter up through the artery to the aorta. The thin space between the two tubes is where gas is pumped back and forth to inflate and deflate the balloon.

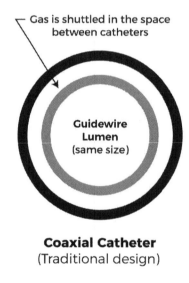

Coaxial Catheter
(Traditional design)

Cross Section of a Typical Intra-Aortic Balloon Catheter

The way it's used can be explained simply too. I purposely say, "explained simply," because reading and doing are two different things—especially when it comes to inserting something near the heart! But basically, the catheter is inserted into the patient through the femoral artery located in the groin area, and the length of the catheter is then snaked up through the femoral artery until the end with the hot dog-size balloon is inside the patient's aorta. The back end that's outside the patient is then hooked up to a pump that's about the size of a microwave oven, which inflates and deflates the hot dog-size balloon.

By inflating and deflating the balloon in the aorta, and syncing the inflation and deflation to a patient's beating heart, the blood flow through the body is significantly improved. In fact, it can be a lifesaver. Sometimes IABs remain in a patient for days or weeks, while waiting for the patient's heart to get stronger.

Here were the challenges. When a catheter is inserted into an artery, it also obstructs the blood flow through that artery. That's not good, especially if the person already has a weak or damaged heart. So there was the goal of decreasing the diameter of the catheter. There was also the challenge to increase the area for the gas to shuttle back and forth (that thin area between the inside tube and the outside tube). More area for the gas flow would allow the balloon to inflate/deflate faster, and that would improve pumping more blood.

So those were two necessary goals.

1. Reduce the outside diameter of the catheter (so the artery is less obstructed).

2. Increase the area between the two catheters (to allow more gas flow).

Easy, right?

Hold on, there were also a few major limitations at the time, basically due to the existing material science. These also need to be the ground rules for your thinking.

- The inner catheter had to remain round and the same size (because the guide wire was already as small as possible.

- The wall thicknesses of the two tubes couldn't be made any thinner.

- The large catheter had to remain round.

So with those goals and limitations in mind—you can go ahead and think about how best to solve the problem.

Before I show you the answer, let me make a few suggestions that might be helpful when approaching a problem where a solution is not obvious.

1. Start with blank paper.

    Sometimes it helps to consider the problem without being overly fixated on the existing design. Existing designs often end up hitting a wall due to inherent limitations, and a new approach needs to be considered. Two blades on a razor might be better than one, but at some point, adding more blades doesn't help. A propeller can only move a plane so fast, so a jet engine had to be invented to go faster.

This is the "blank paper" thinking that resulted in the world's largest taxi company owning no vehicles (Uber), and the world's largest accommodation provider owning no real estate (Airbnb).

2. Break the problem into its simplest definition.
   It's a good idea to describe the problem (or need) simply. And don't include what you presume to know are the associated problems with a particular solution.

   It's like when the team at Apple worked for weeks to prepare a presentation to show Steve Jobs, which included many pages of prototype screenshots showing the new program's functions as to how the app would work. According to Mike Evangelist, who was on the team responsible for coming up with ideas for a DVD-burning program, "Then Steve comes in [to the meeting]. He doesn't look at any of our work. He picks up a marker and goes over to the whiteboard. He draws a rectangle. 'Here's the new application,' he says. 'It's got one window. You drag your video into the window. Then you click the button that says BURN. That's it. That's what we're going to make.'"[27]

3. Ask for Ideas
   The reason we've all heard that "ideas can come from anywhere" is because it's true. Ask for ideas.

4. Involve an Outsider
   I was thinking of titling this point as "Be an Outsider," and that's a good mindset to apply sometimes. Though it can be difficult to forget what you know. It's easier to involve others with a unique perspective. That's an advantage people have from other industries. It's why Nike has no issues hiring people outside of the shoe and apparel industry. Innovators bring what they've learned from across the continuum of their experiences and apply it to the situation at hand.

Before I show you how John Lucas and the professor cleverly solved the problem—and assuming you haven't figured it out yet—go ahead and review the two goals (and the restrictions). What would you do?

Now, back to John Lucas and the professor. I will tell you this. John Lucas and the professor cleverly reduced the overall diameter, thereby providing less obstruction in the artery, and simultaneously increased the area for the gas flow, thereby providing greater volume for the balloon to inflate/deflate more efficiently. The new design went on to generate over $1 billion in sales. More important, their work benefitted many patients. It was a pleasure to have these guys as colleagues.

All right, I'll show you how John Lucas and the professor solved the problem.

In the figure, the original design is shown on the left; the new design is shown on the right. The breakthrough was realizing they could essentially combine the two catheters—and actually share a common wall. Simple. Clever. Ingenious. It was as though they shifted the bullseye. (I gave a little hint in the title of this chapter.)

Note, the illustrations are representational only—in reality, the outer diameter of the new design was smaller than the outer diameter of the old design, so it provided less obstruction to blood flow in the artery. At the same time, the area available to shuttle gas back and forth was increased, which allowed the balloon to inflate/deflate faster, increasing blood pumping efficiency.

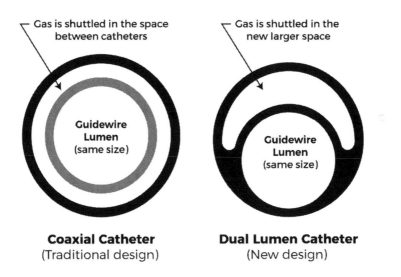

Cross Section of a Traditional Coaxial Design on Left,
and the New Dual Lumen Design on Right

Their clever work produced a win-win, which resulted in countless dub-dubs. The tin man would be proud.

Turnaround Test

A friend of mine swears this is a true story, and I believe him. It happened to him and his wife. After finally getting their van loaded with suitcases, a tent, and a cooler for the family vacation, they gave a final call for their three kids to pile in. The highway was beckoning. The family road trip was about to begin!

Within just a few minutes, and after traveling barely a mile down the road, they realized they'd left one of their kids at home. They immediately turned around to get the stranded boy. He was safe and sound, watching television in the room where they'd last seen him, oblivious to missing the departure.

That's an example of passing the turnaround test. I've never had to go back and pick up a forgotten child, but at one time or another, I have left behind numerous things that necessitated my turning around.

The turnaround test is actually a good qualitative indicator for how much your product is needed and loved by your customers. When they realize it's been left behind, do they love it enough to do an about-face? Or do they think, "No biggie, I can do without."

Does your product pass the turnaround test? Passing can be accomplished for a couple of different reasons. For one, it may be absolutely necessary. A good example would be your wallet or passport. If you're traveling internationally, it's not an option to leave your passport at home.

The other reason for passing the turnaround test, and the one relevant for product developers and marketers, is because the product "feels" absolutely necessary to the owner. It provides so much utility, convenience, and outright enchantment that it's worthwhile making a U-turn. You just don't want to be without it. Products that pass the turnaround test are those that have the best chance of wildly succeeding. They're the products that give more than they get. Those you tell your friends about.

Passing the turnaround test is not magic, though it is elusive. And, if you rely on dumb luck to achieve it, you won't. Instead, if you want a chance of your product or service reaching that rarified level, you'll need to plan for it through design and forethought.

Everything matters, and that combination of factors includes the following.

1. Quality. We know quality when we see it reflected in the craftsmanship, the design, and the usage. Management expert Peter Drucker said it well.

> *"Quality in a product or service is not what the supplier puts in. It is what the customer gets out and is willing to pay for. A product is not quality because it is hard to make and costs a lot of money, as manufacturers typically believe. That is incompetence. Customers pay only for what is of use to them and gives them value. Nothing else constitutes quality."*[28]

2. Functionality. Does your product or service let customers do things they couldn't do before? Does it provide new capability? Does it give them what seems like superpowers?

3. Ease of use. Simplicity is necessary for mass adoption. Think "point-and-shoot" cameras. Is your product or service incredibly easy to use? Could an elderly relative use it?

4. Value. There's a saying in project management, "You can mostly do anything; it's just a question of spending time and money." To pass the turnaround test, your product typically has to do the opposite. It has to clearly save time and money.

5. Utility. The dictionary defines utility as "the state of being useful or beneficial." It's a combination of the above and more. Like a machete in a jungle, or a Wet Ones wipe for cleaning ice cream from a little face, your offering needs to be simply useful.

6. Beauty. For a product to be loved, it should be aesthetically pleasing. People are drawn to beauty, and there's not enough of it in the world. Jony Ive, chief designer at Apple, said, "I think we are surrounded by

hundreds and thousands of products that show companies don't care enough about what they design for consumers."[29]

If you work ruthlessly to create a product that passes the turnaround test, you have at least a chance of making a product that people truly want and happily use—even if they have to go back to get it.

The Woman Whose Magic Is Five Times Stronger Than Steel

"Any sufficiently advanced technology is indistinguishable from magic."
—Arthur C. Clarke

E very kid in the fifth grade class saw the magic happen. Their teacher had invited a guest visitor to the classroom that day. The guest was an elderly woman, and she captivated the student's attention like a virtuous sorceress holding court.

Her name was Ms. Kwolek, and it was apparent to the students when she entered the room, that she was wise and kind. Ms. Kwolek began by sharing memories from her childhood, many years in the past, when she herself was the age of the students. Ms. Kwolek spoke of her interest in nature and exploring outdoors. She spoke of being curious. And while she was talking, Ms. Kwolek had beside her a glass beaker containing a mysterious liquid.

The kids listened intently and leaned forward to get a closer look at the magic that was about to happen. Picking up a glass rod that was about the size of a pencil, and using it like a magic wand, Ms. Kwolek carefully extended it into the beaker and gently touched the surface of the liquid. Then, she slowly lifted the rod from the liquid's surface. And … a long continuous rope began to emerge from the liquid.

It looked like magic. And it didn't happen in a flash or with puff of smoke. The transformation from a liquid into a rope took place in a more astounding manner. It happened s l o w l y. And, inch-by-inch, the rope emerged from the liquid under the observant gaze of the students. The growing length of rope was slowly wrapped around a spool. Ms. Kwolek was like a sorceress, leisurely pulling one rabbit after another from a glass container. The grade schoolers were wide-eyed at the magic. And rightly so.

The feat Ms. Kwolek demonstrated that day has saved thousands of lives; it's used in thousands of products and in dozens of industries. The rope she created from the liquid is used in automobiles, ships, consumer products, building material, tires, bridge reinforcement, armored vehicles, and even in spaceflight.

Born in 1923, Stephanie Kwolek was raised outside Pittsburgh, Pennsylvania, and grew up with a genuine love of nature that she attributed to her father, who was a naturalist. She also had a strong interest in fashion and fabric design, which she credited to her mother.

With the intent of becoming a doctor, Stephanie completed her bachelor of science degree in chemistry from Margaret Morrison Carnegie College in 1946. Needing to earn money before she was able to continue with her medical degree, Kwolek made the pragmatic decision to get a job in the chemical industry for a couple of years.

At the time, the country was fighting World War II, and there was a resulting shortage of men at DuPont. The company needed talented resources, so Kwolek was interviewed by William Hale Charch, a DuPont researcher, who was duly impressed. Charch explained that the hiring process typically took a couple of weeks before an offer would be formalized.

Believing DuPont to be a place where she could make a contribution, Kwolek politely informed Charch that if he wanted to hire her, DuPont should be prompt, because she was considering another offer. Charch typed up the job offer while she waited. It was a good move for all concerned. Kwolek found the research and applied chemistry work at DuPont to be of great interest, and she decided not to pursue a career as a physician.

After several years, and with the anticipated looming shortage of gasoline due to the war, Kwolek was tasked with exploring new formulations to increase material strength, as the company was looking for a material that could be used in tires. Working in the lab one day, Kwolek produced a batch of liquid polymer that appeared cloudy and not viscous. She later remarked that the polymer was cloudy, like the color of buttermilk, and unlike normal polymer formulations that were clear. For that reason, it appeared to have not formulated properly. Normally, the bad mix would have just been tossed into the trash. But, for whatever reason, Kwolek decided to run some tests of this strangely colored solution on a spinneret machine.

However, the technician operating the test machine had a strong hunch that this opaque concoction would likely clog the machine, resulting in a major cleanup mess. So, initially, he argued against doing the tests. But Kwolek persisted, and the tests were run.

The test results were stunning. The material showed dramatically increased tensile strength. The potential for this material was immediately apparent to Kwolek and to DuPont management. DuPont promptly assigned a team to explore applications. Kwolek continued her experimenting and went on to discover that the material could be made even stronger by subjecting it to additional heat treatment. In fact, this material was five times stronger than steel.

DuPont named the new material Kevlar. And Kevlar has made DuPont billions of dollars. Stephanie Kwolek was recognized as a pioneering innovator and received several awards and honors.

Here are some lessons from this innovative wizard.

1. Show flexibility.

   Stephanie Kwolek fully intended to work at DuPont for a couple of years, earn some money, and then attend medical school. But she found herself on a path that aligned with her evolving interests and where she could contribute.

   We're all building on our past experiences. Which is why it's vital that we continue gathering and learning from a variety of experiences. In his commencement address to Stanford University graduates, Steve Jobs said, "You can't connect the dots looking forward; you can only connect them looking backward. So you have to trust that the dots will somehow connect in your future."[30]

2. Push forward.

   We might think it shortsighted that the technician didn't want to test the new, cloudy material because it looked like it'd clog the machine. But the reality is, that's human nature. We might have been inclined the same way. How often are we unconsciously predisposed to resist doing new work that ostensibly appears to be without opportunity? Or worse yet, would also require us to do a major cleanup.

3. Experiment (make mistakes).
   Stephanie Kwolek didn't intentionally formulate the batch of polymers
   that became Kevlar. She was simply trying various formulations and
   producing material outside the typical temperature range. The initial
   result looked like a failed formulation. It was Kwolek's willingness
   to try some things that previously had not been done that led to the
   discovery.

   "All sorts of things can happen when you're open
   to new ideas and playing around with things."
   —Stephanie Kwolek

4. Get help.
   Once the discovery was made, DuPont wasted no time in getting other
   people involved with Kevlar. It was this dramatic increase in resources
   that allowed the rapid exploitation and application of Kevlar into a
   wide-range of industries and products.

5. Release it to the world.
   Making the raw material available to any company allowed for the
   real-world applications to increase geometrically. It's why Kevlar
   is used in applications from fiber optic cables to Reebok CrossFit
   clothing to a key shielding component of the modules for the
   International Space Station.

   "I guess that's just the life of an inventor: what people
   do with your ideas takes you totally by surprise."
   —Stephanie Kwolek

   How many applications are there for a material that's five times
   the strength of steel? More than anyone one person could determine.
   Release it to the world.

6. Inspire and teach.
   Like her parents instilled in her an interest in design and nature as
   a child, Stephanie Kwolek had a passion for inspiring and educating
   children as to the wonders of science. She frequently spoke to middle
   schoolers about her work.

Joyce Bedi, a senior historian at the Smithsonian Lemelson Center for the Study of Invention and Innovation, said of Kwolek, "She was a wonderful person and an inspiration to many, especially young women interested in science and invention."[31]

"Even in my neighborhood, the kids come to me for interviews for their term papers. I ask them later what grades they got, and they're always A-pluses."
—Stephanie Kwolek

7. Make magic.
   Of course, there's no guarantee you'll "make magic" in your work. But that's a good goal.

"I tell young people to reach for the stars. And I can't think of a greater high than you could possibly get than by inventing something."
—Stephanie Kwolek

There's magic all around us waiting to be discovered. We just need to be courageous in our attempt to uncover it, and then to develop it. Go pull a rabbit out of a hat.

Ladies and Gentlemen, the Greatest of All Inventors Is ...

It'd be difficult to name the greatest of all inventors. But someone did. And it's difficult to argue with the choice. Sure, so many possibilities come to mind. Thomas Edison (light bulb, phonograph); Grace Hopper (computer); Shirley Jackson (telecommunications); Steve Jobs. Or maybe it was the person who invented the wheel. Nope, nope, nope, nope, and no. Mark Twain named the "greatest of all inventors." And his choice was present with everyone on the aforementioned list.

So, who then is the greatest inventor of all time? Here's a short story containing a clue.

Donald Stookey was born in small town called Hay Springs, Nebraska. As a young man, he graduated from the Massachusetts Institute of Technology (MIT) with a doctoral degree in physical chemistry. After graduation, he had a couple of decent (though different) job offers. One of his offers was from the Nabisco Baking Company and the other was from Corning Glass.

He thought about what he wanted to be doing in his future and couldn't quite imagine a career making bread, so he took the job with Corning. Stookey went to work in the Corning research and development (R&D) department. He had no experience with glass at that point, so he began experimenting and learning about the material. It was during one such experiment that Stookey thought he'd ruined one of the ovens in the Corning laboratory.

Stookey had placed a piece of glass in the oven, intending to heat it to 600 degrees F. But, when he came back to the laboratory to check on the glass, he realized the oven controls were broken and saw the temperature gauge was holding steady at 900 degrees F. In a rush, he quickly grabbed a pair of tongs and pulled the glass from the oven. Being in a hurry, he had a poor grip on the glass, and watched it slip from the tongs and crash onto the hard, concrete floor.

But it didn't shatter. Instead, Stookey said, "The thing bounced and didn't break. It sounded like steel hitting the floor."[32] Stookey didn't know it at the time, but he'd accidentally invented glass ceramics. Turns out the material had never-before-seen properties. So he spent several more years working on the material, before Corning announced it to the world as PyroCeram. It was ultrahard, heat resistant, and strong—and perfect for a lot of things. It was used as the nose cone for supersonic missiles, and unlike a metal nose cone, it allowed the radar signals to readily pass through.

Oh, and it also became the cookware product that Corning named CorningWare, which was used in millions of homes in America. It could go from the hot oven into the freezer without cracking. And it wouldn't break, if by chance it landed on the floor. It's estimated that nearly 750 million pieces of CorningWare products have been sold. What's more, decades later the material further evolved into Gorilla Glass, which we're familiar with as the black screen covering iPhones, iPads, and other devices sold around the world.

Donald Stookey had a long and innovative career at Corning. He also invented photochromic glass, which allows for the darkening of sunglasses when exposed to bright lights. Stookey invented photosensitive glass, though this invention was kept confidential for many years. Turns out the military used his invention during World War II to hide messages inside transparent glass, which could only be read when heated by the recipient.

Donald Stookey went on to work for 47 years at Corning and earned over 60 patents. So, was Donald Stookey the "greatest inventor of all time"?

Nope. At least not according to Mark Twain (though Twain, of course, lived long before Stookey and some of the other inventors mentioned).

On that topic to name the greatest of all inventors, Mark Twain said, "Accident."

And sure enough, if you study innovation and invention, you'll find "accident" is commonly present.

Thirteen Ways to Innovate (and Avoid Being Eaten by a Giant Bird)

I t's hard to know when the best era was to be an innovator. Maybe we missed it. There was certainly a lot of opportunity for innovation 2.6 million years ago. That's the period when anthropologists dated the earliest actual tools ever found, which were simple modified stone tools, such as a hand axe. So, except for the chipped stone, that would have left basically ... let me think, everything else to be invented.

Of course not everything would have been conducive to living the life of an inventor back then. For one thing, there wasn't even language. Good luck using grunts to describe plans for a steam engine. And before you could even begin to make a drawing, you'd have to invent paper and pencils. Paper, I think, is made somehow with trees and glue, so you'll have to also invent glue. And I have no idea how to make a pencil. My suggestion is to start with a chipped rock.

As for the office environment, it would be fairly hostile because you'd be mostly outdoors. Keep an eye out for the Titanis—a large, flightless, carnivorous bird that was over eight feet tall and weighed 330 pounds—and the Megalodon—which happened to be the largest shark that ever lived and could weigh 100 tons and reached 20 meters long. So, while the era was definitely ripe for innovation, it would have been really hard to fight a gigantic shark with a hand axe the size of an iPhone (you see, I'm already introducing technology to the Pliocene epoch).

Which brings us to today. The good news is that we're here, with language, paper, and computers; and we have the perspective of 2.6 million years of history to comprehend just how far innovation has moved the world forward. Often, it does so in small ways (a pointy rock is more effective than a blunt rock) and sometimes in big ways (smelting metals is a way to make better tools).

And here's what we see. Whether innovation involved fashioning the first stone tools millions of years ago or powering pumps with early steam engines in 1781, the advances never ceased and continually improved our ability to survive.

It's also apparent that we're living in a period where innovation is occurring at a rate not previously experienced. Back in the day, your brand new stone axe looked just like your great-great-grandpa's old-school stone axe. Today kids aren't happy tweeting with their great-great-grandpa's telegraph.

Indeed, it's the nature of humankind to create and invent, and that has profoundly shaped our world and lives. Inventing and creating is fundamental to being human. Yet, many people probably don't see themselves as innovators; or they believe that creativity isn't a necessary part of their work.

Maybe your job involves just keeping the wheels on the business by managing the day-to-day problems. And when you're heads-down with a manufacturing problem or challenges with vendors, you might not be doing much innovation. That's understandable. But, remember we've come a long way since the stone axe, due in part to continuous innovation; so, do your part or risk becoming food for giant birds or sharks.

Here are some pragmatic ways in which you can innovate.

1. Cross-pollinate.

   Combine things that haven't been used together before. It's what Steve Jobs did when he incorporated various typeface fonts with the computer. I will always remember my amazement (having purchased a Mac in 1984) at being able to select a block of text and change the font to a variety of choices.

   There are infinite ways to cross-pollinate. Even a simple, yet clever, addition can add competitive differentiation. Just look at the Reef sandals that incorporate a bottle opener into the sole.

2. Introduce new technology.

   It's great to run outside in beautiful weather. But I don't mind running outside in terrible weather. That wasn't always the case. I used to come in completely soaked and freezing after running for hours like a lost soul in the freezing rain. Now I come in warm and dry after running like a lost soul in the freezing rain. Thank you, Nike and Gore-Tex.

3. Look forward.
This is how people got rich in the early days of the Web. Some people saw the burgeoning adoption and started Web design companies. When companies wanted websites, those businesses grew. Other people saw the Web as a platform to publish inexpensively and reach an audience of millions for next to free—so they started companies that let people post videos or blogs.

What could you or your company do today to take advantage of how the world will be different in the near future?

4. Look backward.
Sometimes it helps to look at the past. This is basically the opposite of looking forward. If nothing else, looking backward gives you an appreciation for the inevitable march of change, and it will remind you to continually be thinking of improvements, before your competitors. What clues do the past tell you about the future?

Remember what it was like before fax, email or the Web? How did your company adopt those technologies and use them to add value to your customers? What does it portend about how your company will navigate changes in the future?

And, more recently, what about the ubiquity of mobile devices, the availability of cloud computing and the nearly free platforms to let you communicate? How did your business utilize these technologies to add value (or not)?

5. Redesign.
Sometimes, you don't need a revolution. You just need a major evolution, a completely new and improved design. Something that reimagines the product or the offering. This can be difficult for an organization, because people are comfortable with the tried and familiar. A redesign means abandoning the current offering and launching something new.

6. Subtract and delete.
This is the discipline of simplifying or pruning, and is often

overlooked. It involves eliminating those products or services that aren't moving the business forward, yet subtly drain resources from the organization that could otherwise be applied elsewhere.

Spotting them is usually obvious; they're the offerings that contribute little to revenue. Yet getting rid of them is often difficult, as they typically don't involve much time, and are often viewed as things that "round out the line, even though we hardly ever sell them."

The reality is that most everything takes time or resources; and you have to weigh the benefits of spending energy on anything not associated with the future of your company.

7. Ask your customer.
   Get out of the office and visit your top customers (you should be doing that anyway). Ask them what changes to your products or services would help them generate more sales or save time or money.

   Yes, it's true that customers don't always know what they want. Henry Ford supposedly said, "If I had asked my customers what they wanted, they would have said a faster horse." That might be folklore. There were dozens of automobile companies in existence in 1901 when Henry Ford started the Henry Ford Company, so his customers probably would have been able to express an interest in reliable, less expensive automobiles. Most of the time, your customers know what they want, and most of the time you need to listen. Keep track of how many customers tell you nearly the same thing. You can always decide to ignore their requests.

8. Scare yourself.
   It's human nature to worry that there might be a saber tooth tiger above that boulder ready to pounce. That fear has surely kept countless tribe members alive. It could still help you today. It's often easier to imagine what innovative moves a competitor might be working on. Ask yourself, "What could a competitor do that could severely affect my product category or the market?" The exercise might result in your generating valuable ideas for yourself and provide the motivation (fear) to do something.

9. Take a hybrid approach.
   This might seem similar to the first suggestion to cross-pollinate, but that really concerns combining two disparate ideas (fonts and computers, sandals and bottle openers) whereas taking a hybrid

approach implies taking a look at combining two different solutions currently being used in the market. A good example would be hybrid cars, which combine gas engines and electric motors (along with batteries for storage and generating capability).

Another example would be reposable medical instruments, which combines traditional reusable instruments with disposable medical devices. The end result is that the handle is sterilizable and reusable, while the cutting tip would be disposable. Reposable medical instruments have the advantage of reducing waste, cutting costs, and being perfectly sharp and clean for each new patient.

10. Improve the product's essence

What does your product or service actually provide? Figure out what need or needs your offering satisfies and make improvements there. It's often not as obvious as it seems.

Does Starbucks provides a "great cup of coffee"? Or does Starbucks provide a comfortable, clean, familiar environment for people to happily sit and talk or open their laptops and use Wi-Fi to get some work done between appointments?

Does a Rolex watch provide accurate timekeeping (actually, less accurate than a $10 quartz watch), or does it provide a recognizable brand to which the wearers want to be associated?

11. Innovate your marketing and sales.

Sometimes the innovation doesn't need to be with your product but rather with your marketing. Do prospects understand your value proposition? How could you improve your messaging? What is the prospect's experience?

At a company where I worked, we switched from a distributor organization to a direct sales organization that consisted primarily of nurse practitioners. We transformed the sales process to focus on education (the science of healing), the patient (clinical outcomes), and physician benefit (decreased complications). The product was already sufficiently superior to other products in the market, so the only changes were to the marketing and sales efforts. Worldwide sales skyrocketed, doubling to over 50 percent market share within 18 months.

12. Empower your customers.

What can you do to empower your customers to help grow your

business? Are they able to play a part in your growth? Can you enlist thought leaders to discuss the benefits of what you offer to their colleagues?

13. Change the usage.

Another possibility is to consider expanding the customer usage patterns for your product. Arm & Hammer lists hundreds of uses for baking soda on its website and includes categories like pets, baby, outdoors, and personal care. Ironically, I didn't even see baking listed as a use.

While there are many other ideas for ways to innovate, these will provide some good ideas to get you started. Honestly, you'll do great. And I'm not just saying that to make you feel good. Here's the reality. You come from a family of innovators. In fact, your lineage is incredibly impressive. Every one of your ancestors had to be clever enough and move fast enough to survive. Otherwise, you wouldn't even be here. The ability to innovate is in your genes.

So, pull up a chair, or drag over a rock, and think about what you can improve to create a better future. And don't worry about any eight-foot, carnivorous, 330-pound birds. I'm inventing an app for that.

Evolve or Die

First, the bad news. Chances are your company is probably going to go under. Whether large and successful, or small and nimble, the odds are your company will remain focused on the business at hand. Chugging forward with its current way of doing business, selling those products and services that have served so well. It works. Sometimes for a long while. Until it doesn't.

"Unlikely," you're saying. "The company has done well for (5, 10, 50) years!"

But, ahead (somewhere) lies a treacherous curve. And because your company is like other companies (comprised of people with habits and needs and shortsightedness), the organization is basically resistant to change—despite the "we think out-of-the-box" platitudes. Senior management doesn't know what it doesn't know. Why should those managers be different from anybody else? And the future has a way of blindsiding most of us with change.

The ironic thing is that the company likely succeeded in the first place because it was innovative and drove change. Yet its successful run makes continued evolution difficult and counterintuitive.

It's easy to find examples of companies that failed to evolve, missed the twists and turns in the journey, and headed into difficulties. Oftentimes, entirely missing the new world order. Like the proverbial buggy whip manufacturers. Decreasing market share. Lost revenue. Oblivion.

Think about companies and industries that were doing exceptionally well … until they weren't—Blockbuster Video, Motorola, Kodak, Blackberry, Sony, Myspace, Xerox, and Polaroid.

And what's the good news? For one, while it's not easy to successfully navigate through the technological and societal changes ahead, neither is it impossible. Some companies are able to reinvent themselves; to move from one business model to another. Even if you're not the one steering the ship, you can be an influencer.

Maybe you can work on a project that's not officially "sponsored." It's not uncommon for dedicated (stubborn) employees to spend a portion of their spare time on skunkworks, until such time that the work matures and the company realizes it needs what you have. It happens in great companies all the time, which is in part why those companies are great—because some of the people pushed ahead and did what they thought needed doing.

Maybe the even better "good news" is that you are not your company. While it's hard to influence a company's direction, you have complete control over yourself. Meaning, you're free to study what's happening around you and not be one of the many people holding the buggy whip inventory when nobody's buying.

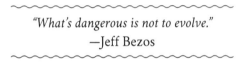

"What's dangerous is not to evolve."
—Jeff Bezos

Change means doing things that are new, and forgoing things that are familiar. It means discomfort and uncertainty, and the real likelihood of being wrong. All in all, it's scary. It really comes down to a decision. You either ride things out, fight for the status quo and hope the changes you're sensing are going to slow (they won't), or you think about where the world is headed and change to get yourself there.

The journey is difficult, but the direction is clear. Evolve or die.

From Humble Beginnings: Secrets of World-Class Innovators and Creators

It's a commonly shared thought among many people, though perhaps often not expressed, that major innovation and creativity happen—elsewhere. And by elsewhere, the thinking is, "somewhere other than here." Not in this unremarkable state. Not in this average town. Not at this company, not with my coworkers, not with my job. And the worst thinking of all ... not with me.

This thinking is so common, that sociologists have a name for it. It's called the worse-than-average effect, and it's the human tendency to underestimate one's achievements and capabilities in relation to others. Turns out this effect seems to occur when chances of success are perceived to be rare. If you catch yourself thinking this way, congratulations are in order. Sociologists have determined that people of high ability tend to underestimate their relative competence in comparison to others.

The problem is that having a worse-than-average outlook diminishes innovative and creative thinking. After all, why get started if it probably isn't going to happen? Reality, of course, is different. Innovation and creativity happen wherever people are intent on making a change and having an impact. It happens everywhere, with every kind of person.

Despite the differences in age, sex, location, ethnicity, socioeconomic level, etc., these creators share common characteristics—a communal way of looking at the world and their place in it that underpins their beliefs about innovation and creativity. This thinking should be applied to your creative work.

Here's a big one. Innovation and creativity are far more likely to happen simply by being open to the idea that it *can* happen. That's actually one of the secrets to innovation and creativity—that the expectation of great things being possible (followed by effort) is a precursor to making great things happen. Your expectations are a good barometer for what's possible. It's what Henry Ford meant when he said, "Whether you believe you can do a thing or not, you are right."[33]

We tell ourselves a story about being creative—or not. Then we live our story and do the work creativity requires—or not.

Here are 10 secrets shared by world-class creators that you should take to heart. The people mentioned here have broad, varied backgrounds, yet the characteristics are common among them all.

1. Believe.

Be aware of the story you tell yourself. Even if the story is so buried in your subconscious that you're not even aware it's there.

Frank Lloyd Wright attended only two semesters of college before leaving to find his first job as a draftsman for $8 a week. He learned on the job and was driven by a belief in himself. Wright said, "The thing always happens that you really believe in; and the belief in a thing makes it happen." Wright went on to create over 1,000 structures and a design philosophy that influences architects and builders to this day. He was recognized by the American Institute of Architect as "the greatest American architect of all time."

"I think it is possible for ordinary people to choose to be extraordinary."
—Elon Musk

2. Be brave.

It might seem an unlikely attribute. After all, the likelihood of anyone having to face a terrifying fear is unlikely. That's the tricky thing about bravery; we think of it as necessary only when facing a major threat or recognized enemy. But the small fears, those we're barely aware of, might be just as insidious as those more daunting. Those micro-doubts accumulate as barely heard whispers, until years later, our possibilities have been silenced beneath a chorus of "not today."

J. K. Rowling created a world of magic and intrigue when she wrote the Harry Potter stories. Her work brought joy to millions and Rowling went from living with government-financial assistance to becoming the wealthiest woman in England. She took pen and paper, pushed aside her doubts, and bravely moved forward. Rowling said, "It takes a great deal of bravery to stand up to our enemies, but just as much to stand up to our friends." And bravery is a habit that builds. Rowling wrote, "You sort of start thinking anything's possible if you've got enough nerve."

Phil Knight ran middle distances for the University of Oregon track team. Knight and his inventive coach, Bill Bowerman, started a small running shoe company called Blue Ribbon Sports—it later became Nike.

"Dare to take chances, lest you leave your talent buried in the ground."
—Phil Knight

3. Keep moving forward.
Failure. Everybody fails. Repeatedly. If there ever was a common theme, it's this. Every wildly innovative person has failed time and time again. And then, they kept learning and kept moving forward, relentlessly pursuing their objectives.

Business magnate Richard Branson said, "You don't learn to walk by following rules. You learn by doing, and by falling over." If you want to succeed, keep moving forward.

4. Practice.
Researcher and author Dr. Anders Ericsson has spent a stellar career studying the acquisition of expert performance. He's the person responsible for what's generally known as the 10,000-hour rule, related to the importance of deliberate practice.

Ericsson wrote, "The differences between expert performers and normal adults are not immutable, that is, due to genetically prescribed talent. Instead, these differences reflect a lifelong period of deliberate effort to improve performance."[34]

That's decades of highly impactful scientific research in a single sentence. Becoming an expert is not due to genetics; it's due to deliberate practice. It's hard, time-consuming work. And no one ever created great work without spending untold hours developing and honing their skills. Which is why the true creative or innovator stands out. A small percentage of people are willing to do the work.

The artist Banksy noted, "All artists are willing to suffer for their work. But why are so few prepared to learn to draw?"

5. Get started now.
Innovators don't wait for the magic to happen. They get started. American artist and photographer Chuck Close knows about building from where you are. He has a rare condition known as prosopagnosia, which makes him unable to recognize faces. Yet his large-scale portraiture works hang in galleries around the world and sell for several million dollars.

"Inspiration is for amateurs. The rest of us just show up and get to work. If you wait around for the clouds to part and a bolt of lightning to strike you in the brain, you are not going to make an awful lot of work. All the best ideas come out of the process; they come out of the work itself."
—Chuck Close

6. Look for simplicity.
Look at any masterpiece, and you'll find there's a lesson in editing. You'd be hard pressed to find a more successful company than Google, or a simpler homepage. Apple products are noteworthy for the simple design philosophy espoused by Steve Jobs and Jony Ive.

And it's not just technology products that benefit from simplicity. Frank Lloyd Wright revealed that "An architect's most useful tools are an eraser at the drafting board, and a wrecking bar at the site."

7. Be bold.
Serial entrepreneur Peter Thiel asks a great question about multiyear plans. His question is, "Why couldn't you do it in six months?" Of course, not everything can be done in six months. But it is a bold and valuable question. Is the timeline really more about the story we're telling ourselves?

X Prize founder Peter Diamandis and his coauthor Steven Kotler explored the topic of striving for bold work in their book, *Bold: How to Go Big, Create Wealth, and Impact the World*. Diamandis said, "Lots of people dream big and talk about big bold ideas but never do anything.

I judge people by what they've done. The ratio of something to nothing is infinite. So just do something."

8. **Help people.**
People innovating and creating are, by definition, focused on bringing something new to the world. Whether producing a product, process, painting, or poem, the goal is to have an impact on others. We're living in a connected world, and you can reach a large number of people with your work, and they can collectively reach an even larger number of people. That's how good work spreads. But, only if it's worth spreading. Only if it benefits people in some way.

It's how technology entrepreneur Mark Zuckerberg describes the fundamental mission of Facebook. "The thing that we are trying to do at Facebook is just help people connect and communicate more efficiently."

Helping people is exactly how Jack Ma, the founder of one of the world's largest retailers, described his company Alibaba. "My job is to help more people have jobs."

9. **Stay curious; stay hungry.**
Curiosity and hunger are the twin forces of creativity. They are the reasons Spanish painter Pablo Picasso explored new periods of painting and sculpting throughout his life and left a legacy in various styles—Blue Period, Rose Period, cubism, neoclassicism, surrealism.

Staying curious requires a sincere appreciation and humbleness in regard to the possibilities before you. And that recognition drives the appetite to continue developing.

Take it from two successful people.

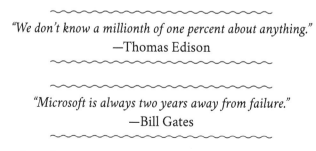

"We don't know a millionth of one percent about anything."
—Thomas Edison

"Microsoft is always two years away from failure."
—Bill Gates

10. **Say yes; have fun.**
Richard Branson said it best. "Life is a helluva lot more fun if you say yes rather than say no."

Garbage In, a Billion Dollars Out

Of all the places you might search for ideas and inspiration for your new innovative product, chances are you wouldn't look in the garbage. But here's a true story where some stale tortillas tossed into the trash led to a product that sells approximately $5 billion annually. It begins exactly where dreams should begin—in Disneyland.

A couple of years after Disneyland opened in 1953 in Anaheim, California, Elmer Doolin, founder of the Frito Company (which merged in 1961 with H. W. Lay and Company to become Frito-Lay) convinced Walt Disney to let him open a Mexican-themed restaurant. Walt agreed, and the restaurant, Casa de Fritos, opened in 1955 in Disneyland. Fritos were provided free to patrons and were featured in several of the meals.

The tortillas used by the restaurant were purchased from a local food producer, Alex Foods, located several miles from Disneyland. One day, a salesman from Alex Foods was checking on inventory at the restaurant, when he noticed there were a lot of stale tortillas tossed in the garbage. The salesman suggested that instead of throwing out the tortillas, the cook should fry them and turn them into chips. That's exactly what the cook did, and over the next several months, these tasty, seasoned chips became extremely popular with Casa de Fritos customers.

Several years after the Frito-Lay merger, a new vice president of marketing, Arch West, visited Casa de Fritos, where he noticed the popularity of the chips. After eating the chips, West thought they might be a new and successful product for Frito-Lay. West pitched the idea, and the new product idea was met with disinterest. So Arch West conducted some preliminary market research that helped him validate interest in the product. He then convinced Frito-Lay, in 1964, to begin marketing the chips, named Doritos.

The rest, as they say, is history. Doritos sales are an estimated $5 billion dollars annually and have been prominently featured for decades in Super Bowl advertisements.[35] In 2008, it was the first extraterrestrial advertisement that was pulsed out over a six-hour period from high-powered EISCAT European space station radars in the Arctic Circle while aimed toward a solar system 42 lightyears from Earth in the Ursa Major constellation. Not bad for an idea that originated from some thrown-out, stale tortillas.

So, the next time you're having some Doritos, be reminded of its unceremonious path to the top and the lesson that there are opportunities everywhere.

PART THREE

Business and Work

Tools of Trade, More Than a Job

Find What You Love
and Let It Kill You

There's a beautiful piece of writing by pianist James Rhodes, which after reading several times I'm only now beginning to truly appreciate. It's a heartfelt request to forgo at least some of the trite, habitual activities that inhabit part of our days. He reminds us to recall our childhood dreams or adult aspirations, kick aside the inertia (fear) of getting started and steadfastly carve out the time to pursue, struggle, and suffer for a goal.

"We seem to have evolved into a society of mourned and misplaced creativity. A world where people have simply surrendered to (or been beaten into submission by) the sleepwalk of work, domesticity, mortgage repayments, junk food, junk TV junk, everything, angry ex-wives, ADHD kids and the lure of eating chicken from a bucket while emailing clients at 8pm on a weekend."[36]

Later in his thoughtful article, Rhodes makes an argument for us to consider going after our dreams. He tells us that the pursuit will likely be ridiculously difficult and time-consuming. It will be exceedingly frustrating and, in the end, might only result in the internal satisfaction of doing something you couldn't do before. And yet, he suggests that alone is often a sufficiently small miracle and satisfaction enough.

In the case of James Rhodes, after ten years of not playing the piano, he left his corporate job and spent the next five years with no income, practicing six hours a day. He lost his wife, 35 pounds, and spent nine months in a mental institution. Was it worth it? He says it was for him. Have a listen to him playing the piano.[37]

A caveat. By no means am I advocating that anyone commit to a life of ruin. But, at the same time, at least for me, Rhodes' words are a reminder that we should embolden ourselves to at least consider chasing down and running to ground an abandoned dream. There's something romantic and appealing in that quest.

Let Rhodes be a great reminder to reach further toward what calls us—whether our loves, our work, or our art. Whether that's family, career, or something else. It's easy to lose yourself in the day-to-day. The mind-numbing, never-ceasing focus of "keeping the wheels" on a job. Doing more with less. Going with the flow. Grinding through uninspired.

Maybe we need to take some inspiration from the unorthodox, the unreasonable ones. The people like James Rhodes wrenching themselves into a new form. The people described in the Apple ad: "Here's to the crazy ones." And that's what I think is meant by the term, "Find what you love and let it kill you." Commit to doing great work, and invest your life force.

Lots of people have done it. They've given us these lessons along the way.

1. The benefit of doing.

   George Bernard Shaw wrote, "A life spent making mistakes is not only more honorable, but more useful than a life spent doing nothing." Good advice from a Nobel Prize winner whose plays continue to be performed more than 100 years after having been written.

   Comedian and author Ruby Wax wasn't afraid of doing. She put together a comedy show called "Losing It," which she started out performing for small audiences within mental institutions. Eventually she took it on the road and invited doctors to attend so they could help audience members who needed mental help.

   Ruby Wax suffered from severe depression and wanted to better understand why. A doctor told her it'd be too difficult for her to understand, so Ms. Wax enrolled in Oxford University and got a master's degree on the topic of neuroplasticity. It was this knowledge that she humorously credits with helping manage her life.

2. Get comfortable with discomfort.

   No explanation needed.

3. Art for art's sake.

   Some people are overly focused on an end result. Vincent van Gogh painted over 800 paintings in his lifetime, and although he tried to sell, sell, sell … he only sold a *single* painting during his lifetime. His work was so underappreciated, that a painting van Gogh gave to a physician in lieu of payment, was used by the doctor to cover a hole in the roof of a chicken coop. Even the work of children typically makes it to exhibit on the refrigerator.

4. Borrow and steal.
   John Cleese, the beloved British writer, comedian, and producer, encourages those involved in creative pursuits (each of us) to start out by imitating those you admire. Cleese says it's how to best learn your craft and how to find your own unique voice.

5. Believe in yourself.
   Despite his intense passion, van Gogh wrote forlornly to his brother, Theo, "A great fire burns within me, but no one stops to warm themselves at it, and passers-by only see a wisp of smoke."

6. Creative work doesn't require great funding.
   Artist Robert Rauschenberg lived in New York City on Fulton Street in 1953 and was obsessed with making art. Some days he lived on 15 to 25 cents a day. There was no money to buy art supplies, so Rauschenberg would walk the neighborhood streets searching for whatever trash he could utilize as art. One day, without money to buy a blank canvas, Rauschenberg found an old quilt that had been thrown out. He used it as a canvas and decided to utilize other materials. That led to his practice of combining a variety of found objects and materials into works he called "Combines," and a new form of art evolved.

> *"I wanted something other than what I could make myself and I wanted to use the surprise and the collectiveness and the generosity of finding surprises. And if it wasn't a surprise at first, by the time I got through with it, it was."*
> —Robert Rauschenberg

7. Creativity takes courage.
   Artist Henri Matisse said exactly that: "Creativity takes courage."

8. Persistence matters.

   From what I can tell, most everyone who's succeeded has overcome "failure." Walt Disney was fired at 22 for not being creative enough, and one of his first ventures went bankrupt. Elon Musk invested his entire $200 million fortune and was on the edge of bankruptcy before SpaceX and Tesla Motors began to slowly get traction and turnaround. Henry Ford failed at the first three automotive companies he founded, before starting a fourth time with the Ford Motor Company.

9. Reinvent.

   Creative people form themselves through the cauldron of passion and practice, and, once successful, they typically continue to reinvent out of bravery or lunacy or both.

   Although Robert Rauschenberg lived for a time on 15 cents a day, eventually his work was critically recognized and his work was highly sought (and highly valued). Yet, in 1964, when Rauschenberg won an international award in Venice, he called his assistant in New York and said to destroy all of his silkscreens so that he wouldn't repeat himself. Such was his commitment to continually search for new artistic frontiers.

> *"To be an artist you have to give up everything,*
> *including the desire to be a good artist."*
> —Jasper Johns

10. Enjoy the journey.

    It's a Taoist saying. It's a Chinese proverb. And Steve Jobs popularized the phrase in our time.

    We're here for the briefest of time. We're each going from our own point A to point Z—with peaks and valleys, stops and starts—along the way.

Create. Be kind. Be courageous. Love. Enjoy. It's what makes us human. I love you.

Proven Strategies on How to Create a Hit

Here's a short story about the possibilities of success or failure, and the factors and randomness that go into deciding the outcome.

Joanne is a young, single mom who writes her first book, and then finds an agent who agrees to try to help find a publisher. The book is sent to a publisher for review, and shortly thereafter rejected. This is repeated again and again by Joanne and her agent, each time the submission is met with a rejection. In fact, it's repeated twelve times, before a publisher was found who agreed to publish the book—and only because the daughter of the company's chairman liked the book.

Since the publication of her first book, *Harry Potter and the Philosopher's Stone*, the author Joanne Rowling, or J. K. Rowling as she is better known, and her books have gained immense popularity and become a cultural worldwide phenomenon, selling more than 500 million copies and being translated into over 80 languages (as of 2018). J. K. Rowling has subsequently become one of the richest women in the world. Yet the publication of her first book might well never have happened.

The road to creating a hit—whether a book, movie, product, or company—requires a significant amount of work and passion. History and recent research also show that creating a hit can be unpredictable and involve a good amount of luck. Yet there are a couple of simple proven strategies that individuals and companies can use that have been shown to have a profound effect on making a hit. In fact, one of the companies successfully using these strategies has created hit after hit after hit. They've released 20 major products over the past 23 years, and every one of the 20 have been blockbusters, each generating well over $100 million dollars. But more about that later.

To learn more about how to create a hit product, I met with Kartik Hosanagar, a professor at Wharton who has been recognized as one of the top 40 business professors under 40. Hosanagar has his doctoral degree in management science and information systems from Carnegie Mellon University; has received several teaching awards; has done work for Google, Nokia, American Express, Citi; and been involved with a number of tech startups. He's a thoughtful and experienced teacher and entrepreneur. Here is what I learned from Kartik Hosanagar.

1. We are in the era of the hit.

   You're likely familiar with the Pareto principle, or the 80/20 rule. As a quick reminder, it describes that approximately 80 percent of the effects come from 20 percent of the causes. A couple of examples are that approximately 80 percent of the mobile phones are produced by roughly 20 percent of the manufacturers; or that roughly 80 percent of a grocery store's sales come from 20 percent of its customers. While there have always been companies, products, and people who received a disproportionate amount of success, we are now in an era where the disproportion is even greater—where having a successful hit brings more return than ever.

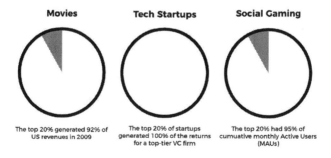

Graph from Prof. Kartik Hosanagar.

Hosanagar explained that the primary reason this is occurring is because of "scalability." He explained that scalability is the reason a movie star makes more money than a teacher—because the product of an actor's work can be readily reproduced, delivered, and enjoyed by millions of people. And just as that winner-takes-all dynamic drives individual compensation scenarios, it also drives revenue concentration in various industries.

Subsequent to hearing Hosanagar's research on the topic, and reading some of his work, the thought occurred to me that another key reason driving the "winner-take-all" era of the hit is "availability." An offering needs to be both readily scalable (such as mass producing widgets) and readily available to tip the scales toward a hit-centric market.

Having people, products, or industries that are scalable and available not only drives a winner-takes-all market dynamic (or at least a winner-takes-a-greatly-disproportionate-amount), but it also means that small differences in quality translate into big differences in market share. As an example, 20 years ago you might have had the choice of driving to a bookstore in your town or to a slightly higher quality bookstore (whatever that means to you) 15 minutes farther away. In that scenario, you likely would just stop locally and save the time, but forgo the slightly better quality atmosphere of the distant store. However, if both bookstores were online, you'd use the online store that provides even a slightly higher quality level, because there is no longer any advantage to use the lower quality option.

This phenomenon can be seen in the graph below. Although any of the search engines would work, there's no disadvantage in using the one with the highest quality, even if that is barely discernible.

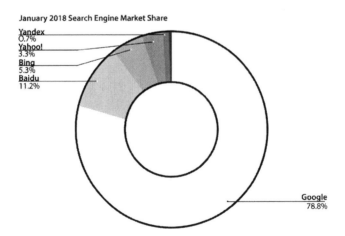

January 2018 Search Engine Market Share

Yandex 0.7%
Yahoo! 3.3%
Bing 5.3%
Baidu 11.2%
Google 78.8%

Scalability can amplify the impact of small differences in quality.

2. There are two big problems in determining hits.
   There is, however, a significant problem with scalability and availability translating into big differences in market share—market predictability becomes difficult. Unpredictability arises because small differences in quality can be difficult to discern and hence their impact on the market can be highly unpredictable.

   Another factor driving unpredictability in markets that are scalable and available is that social media and other social influences will dramatically affect market receptivity and share.

3. What are the inherent qualities of a successful product?
   This was cleverly studied by Matthew Salganik, a sociology professor at Princeton, who wanted to better understand how much of success could be attributed to the inherent qualities of the successful thing itself, and how much was just chance.

   An example is the *Mona Lisa*. The painting is seen by throngs of people daily and kept behind bulletproof glass and guarded by a railing. The question Salganik and others asked is this: "Is the popularity of the painting due to its exquisite quality or some other factors?"

   Salganik constructed a clever experiment where he created a website that contained 48 new songs by unheard of musical artists. He funneled 30,000 teenagers to the website to listen to the songs. After listening, they could download the songs they liked for free. Salganik created nine separate worlds each containing the 48 songs. In eight of the worlds, the teens could see which songs had been downloaded by their peers and how many times, so they knew which songs their peers thought were good. In one of the worlds, Salganik hid which songs had been downloaded, thereby removing any social influences. The 30,000 teenagers were then randomly assigned to each of the nine worlds, so they could listen and then download the songs they liked.

   What was fascinating about the experiment is that different songs became significantly more popular in different worlds. As an example, in one world a song came in first, and in another world, it came in 40 out of 48 total songs. What the experiment showed is that history evolved differently in the different worlds and was influenced by initial social cues, which over time became magnified. Salganik went on to do other similar studies and found that quality does have a limited role, but after meeting a certain level of quality, whether or not it becomes a huge success is basically a matter of chance. A matter of who liked what and how those influences grew.

This randomness certainly seems to have been reflected in the thinking of William Goldman, the American novelist and screenwriter, when he said "Nobody knows anything ... Not one person in the entire motion picture field knows for certainty what's going to work. Every time out it's a guess."

4. Defying the randomness.
    So, if producing a hit is mostly a matter of scalability and availability, and if those two factors inherently make predicting a hit unpredictable, how can you improve your hit prediction? The answer lies in a couple of simple techniques.

    But first, let me tell you about a company that has consistently generated hits. The company that was alluded to at the beginning of this chapter is Pixar Animation Studios. It has had 20 out of 20 hits for Walt Disney pictures. A typical year for any large movie studio has a few movies that do well, but the vast majority underperform and generate no profit for the studio.

    Pixar however defies the odds. Kartik Hosanagar calculated that based on the odds of a 1 in 10 blockbuster success rate, having the first 14 Pixar movies all be hits in a row is actually 1 in a 100 trillion probability! And Pixar has continued to defy the odds. To date, in 2018, Pixar has made 20 major films and each has been a blockbuster.

    So, how does Pixar do it? And how can you employ its practices in your organization.

    Rule number 1. Iterative testing—fail early and often.

    Typically, idea generation, whether for new products or services, is done by a small group of people within an organization—oftentimes this is marketing or product development. Pixar generates its ideas broadly and involves up to 500 different ideas, all boiled down into one sentence pitches. The ideas are mixed and matched and put through several iterations until they are winnowed down to the best concepts. As Lee Unkrich, director of *Toy Story 3* explains, "We fail a lot. We just don't fail by the time the movie comes out."

    Rule number 2. Generate and leverage early momentum.

    As Matt Salganik showed, social influence is critical in creating a hit product. Therefore, it's critical for organizations to do whatever they can to lead and affect the social factors influencing their brands and/or product adoption through authentic engagement with their audiences and influencers.

Social engagement is best done when the spread of the offering is actually a viral part of the user experience, such as the following.

- When you receive a digital holiday card via email where your friend's face is superimposed on the dancing elf, and you're provided with a link that allows you to do the same thing to someone else (and spread the word).

- Online eyeglass frame store Warby Parker (started by former Hosanagar students) that lets customers send photos of themselves trying on different eyeglass frames to their friends to solicit their opinions on what looks best (and spread the word).

- Conference promotion where attendees receive a free book, thereby driving ranking up the *New York Times* bestseller list (and spread the word).

- Creating valuable and low cost (or free) educational content to drive views and membership (Coursera, Udacity, etc.).

5. Influencing the outcome.
    Experience and observation have shown me that oftentimes there seems to be no reasonable or logical explanation for something that has become a hit. Sometimes it seems that popularity is in inverse proportion to its inherent value or quality. There are countless examples, and I'll resist the temptation to start listing examples of things I think inane. But it does seem that for every product or artistic endeavor that was created as a direct result of commitment and obsession with quality—that deserves to be a hit—there is likely an inferior offering that is similar or even more popular.

    Kartik Hosanagar and Matt Salganik have explained some of the reasoning as to why this occurs. More important, they've pointed out a couple of ways in which the randomness of creating a hit can be influenced.

So whether you're working on the next big mobile app, a Marty McFly hoverboard, the next great rock album release (yes, they're still called albums), or developing a new medical device—remember you can significantly improve your odds of success by using the same strategies that helped Pixar deliver 20 hits in a row. Fail early and often, and generate and leverage early momentum. As Buzz Lightyear would say—"To infinity and beyond!"

Ten Things You Need to Know About Work

Some years ago, I asked my friend, Stephen D. Chakwin Jr., to be a guest speaker at a "dine and learn" event for a company where I worked. Stephen is an attorney practicing in the greater New York area. He's intelligent, reflective, and a lifelong learner.

That evening, he spoke earnestly to the group about work, ideas, and the importance of living a meaningful life. I've often thought about that evening, as it was one of those special occasions where everyone was genuinely engaged, the questions sincere, and the group discussion open and honest. There seemed to be a shared understanding among everyone present.

As it turns out, the other day I happened to come across my notes from that evening. The advice is as relevant as ever, and I only wish I'd referred back to the advice more frequently. I'm not sure what sources Stephen used to compile the list—though I suspect it was an accumulation of his experiences, readings, and connections. I'll include a portion of the notes below.

1. No matter what anyone says, you are an independent contractor.

2. You need to market yourself inside and outside your organization.

3. If you can't explain in 50 words or less why you are the best person in the world for the job that you are doing, you might not be doing it for long.

4. If you can't explain in 50 words or less why the company you are working for is the best place in the world for you to be working, you might not be working in the right place.

5. Unless you are oriented horizontally (how the way you work compares with how everyone else does the same thing), vertically (how the way you work fits in with those above and below you in the company hierarchy), and in time (you have a clear idea of where you have come from and where you are heading in your work life), you are going to drift.

6. Always connect with as many people as you can in your industry—the best will teach you a lot, the worst will teach you more.

7. Always connect with as many people as you can outside your industry. Speaking with them about what they do and perceive, and explaining what you do and perceive, will teach you more about what you really do than years of discussions with your colleagues.

8. Your only competition is yourself.

9. If you find work that you like enough to do for a long time, there's a chance that you will last long enough to become good at it.

10. There are two excellent tests of whether you are doing the right work: how you feel on Monday morning and how you feel at the end of the work day.

Thirteen People Who Turned Failure into Success

Maybe the secret to success is to eat dog food. I never thought about eating dog food, but I know someone who did. It was what was necessary to keep his dream alive. You know who he is too.

There have been a couple of times in my life when I had barely any money. During one such time, a friend surprised me and loaded my refrigerator and pantry with groceries. That's something you'll never forget and is guaranteed to make you want to pay it forward by doing it for someone else.

A young person typically has two imagined scenarios about people who are hugely successful. One scenario is that wildly successful people became successful because they're "just awesome." Meaning they were mostly born with a profound and immediately apparent capability, and the world beat a path to their door. The other imagined scenario is that successful people reached greatness because they got extremely lucky, like drawing the winning lottery ticket. Note that neither of the scenarios involves eating dog food.

Maybe, occasionally those scenarios are accurate. But, so far, I haven't been able to find someone extremely accomplished who got there via those paths. If you know of anyone—please let me know. To the contrary, everybody I know who changed the world did so despite a long list of failures and challenges. In fact, it seems everybody's road to success was actually a rocky trail with countless switchbacks and plenty of rockslides.

Here's a typical story. A guy takes his university entrance exam three times before getting in. Then when he starts looking for work, he applies to 30 different jobs and is rejected by all of them. One of the jobs is to work at Kentucky Fried Chicken, which by the way had 24 applicants, and KFC hired 23 of them … but not him. Finally he gets a job teaching English at a university in China for $12 a month. He says he applied to Harvard 10 times, always being rejected. "Nobody said that I would be a very capable person that would do something significant or meaningful in the future," he said. That's the short story of Jack Ma, who in 1999 founded Alibaba and is the richest man in China, worth an estimated $42 billion in 2018.

That brings me back to the dog food.

One of Walt Disney's early jobs was at the *Kansas City Star*, a newspaper from which he was fired because of lack of creativity. Some years later, in 1921, he started an animation company called Laugh-O-Gram Studio, but eventually Disney had to shut the company down. It was during this period, that he could barely pay the rent and resorted to eating dog food. And then, things went downhill from there. In 1926, Disney created a cartoon character named Oswald the Lucky Rabbit. He visited Universal Studios, the cartoon's distributor, where he later found out that Universal secretly patented the character, hired Disney's artists directly, and continued the cartoon without paying him.

The world didn't beat a path to the recognizable talent of Jack Ma or Walt Disney, nor did anyone hand them a ticket to success. There are thousands of examples of people repeatedly failing before they succeeded. Here are twelve examples.

1. Akio Morita

   His first company was called Tokyo Telecommunications Engineering Corporation, which came out with a rice cooker that burnt rice and ended up selling poorly. Rather than making knock-off products like many other Japanese companies, Morita wanted to develop quality innovative companies. He focused on a pocketsize radio. The best he could develop was just a bit too large for a typical pocket; he had his salesmen wear shirts with oversized pockets so the radio would fit. Morita foresaw the importance of branding and changed the name of his company to Sony.

2. Elon Musk

   Musk poured his $200 million payout from PayPal into his next two companies—SpaceX and Tesla Motors. At one point, while teetering on the edge of bankruptcy, Musk debated if he should get rid of one of his companies so the other would succeed. He stuck with both, and the companies slowly made progress (through continual uphill battles). Musk and his team have accomplished the seemingly impossible, as both companies are revolutionizing their respective industries.

3. Thomas Edison
His grade school teachers said he was "too stupid to learn anything." Yet he helped develop many inventions that ushered in the modern age, including the motion picture camera, the phonograph, and a practical light bulb. Edison was also an extraordinary businessman who was an early advocate of mass production and teamwork of innovation, with over 1,000 US patents.

4. Abraham Lincoln
Lincoln had his share of setbacks, including failing in business and failing to get into law school. He suffered from depression, was defeated for nomination to Congress, and was defeated for nomination for vice president. He kept moving forward and was elected president in 1860.

5. Theodor Seuss Geisel
Dr. Seuss' first book, *And to Think That I Saw It on Mulberry Street*, was rejected by 27 publishers. According to Geisel, he was walking home and thinking of burning the manuscript, when he ran into an old friend and classmate who helped him find a publisher. Dr. Seuss went on to sell more than 600 million books, translated into more than 20 languages.

6. Stephen King
His first book, *Carrie*, was rejected 30 times, so King threw it in the trash. His wife rescued the manuscript and told him to keep submitting. King has since published over 64 books (as of 2018), all worldwide bestsellers, having sold more than 350 million copies.

7. J. K. Rowling
At one point, a single mom without a job, Rowling was living off unemployment benefits, had an unfinished book, and two mouths to feed. She was rejected by 12 different publishers and began to lose confidence in her book. Finally, Barry Cunningham, of Bloomsbury Publishing, agreed to publish the book (in part because his eight-year-old daughter liked the first chapter), though Rowling was admonished to get a day job because she wouldn't make any money writing

children's books. She said, "Rock bottom became the solid foundation on which I rebuilt my life."

8. Elvis Presley

   "The King" hardly needs an introduction. Yet when Presley tried out as a vocalist for the Eddie Bond band, Bond rejected him with the advice to stick to driving "because you're never going to make it as a singer." Similarly, Presley was told by Jim Denny, manager of the Grand Ole Opry, "You ain't going nowhere, son. You ought to go back to driving a truck."

9. Oprah Winfrey

   Born in an economically troubled neighborhood and raised by a single, teenage mom, Oprah experienced considerable hardship, including being physically abused as a teenager. Winfrey became a successful media proprietor, talk show host, actress, and philanthropist.

10. Orville and Wilbur Wright

    After several years of building kites and gliders (and numerous crashes), the brothers changed the world on December 17, 1903, when they broke the bounds of gravity and flew a heavier-than-air machine. And this was achieved by two men with no formal engineering training. The two brothers were originally inspired by a toy helicopter that their father brought home and flew around the room. Orville took his father on what was his dad's one and only flight. As Orville gained elevation, his dad enthusiastically yelled out, "Higher, Orville, higher!"

    When Neil Armstrong stepped onto the Moon on July 20, 1969, inside his spacesuit was a piece of fabric from the wing of the original Wright Flyer.

11. Soichiro Honda

    Honda started a machine shop in 1937 to produce piston rings for Toyota, where he labored long hours and even slept in the workshop. To keep things going, he pawned his wife's jewelry. Unfortunately, his product failed to meet Toyota's quality inspection standards and was rejected. Rather than give up, he went back to school and kept working until winning a contract with Toyota two years later.

    As steel was not readily available during the war, he collected surplus gasoline cans discarded by US fighters, calling them "gifts from President Truman," which he used as raw materials for manufacturing. Honda endured his factory being devastated by a bomb and then later being destroyed by an earthquake.

The gasoline shortage after the war resulted in people walking or riding bicycles, so Honda started modifying bicycles by attaching small engines. Honda Motor Company's revenue was $138 billion in 2018.

12. Henry Ford

The first automobile Ford designed was the Quadricycle, which wasn't fit for mass production. Then Ford founded the Detroit Automotive Company, which failed because Ford's perfectionism got the better of him, and he couldn't stop tinkering. Ford had little to show for his work 18 months into the effort, and the company was disbanded.

Ford eventually started the Ford Motor Company and built the Model A. The first cars had so many problems that Ford had to send mechanics throughout the country to fix them. The good news was that the mechanics came back with ideas to improve the cars, and that knowledge went into correcting the future builds. Ford learned that "Failure is simply the opportunity to begin again, this time more intelligently."

Counterintuitive Secrets to Grow Your Career

My dad used to call me "Donkey Number One" when I was a kid. I know that might sound kind of mean, but that really wasn't his intent. I was the oldest, and it was just his way of being funny and probably trying to curtail my overzealous imagination. Like sitting in a small closet pretending I was in a rocket ship, or trying to build a real robot when I was seven or eight. (It was made out of wood boxes so heavy that its legs wouldn't support its own weight. I must have thought it would "walk" by magic … because there were no motors.) So yea, maybe that was kind of "donkey-like."

Don't get the wrong impression; my dad has always been a great guy. Everybody loves him, and I do too. He was the best man at my wedding. Besides, if I occasionally exhibited donkey behavior, well, I'm not alone. There have certainly been a *lot* of people who seem to do things that don't make sense. Maybe occasionally you've done some seemingly irrational things too. Maybe it's not always bad.

Everybody likes to study what looks like winning behaviors. But for every right, there's a left, and you can surely learn a lot from those people who take a counterintuitive approach. It's the people who go against the grain that were celebrated in the Apple "Here's to the crazy ones" campaign. Who knows what percentage of time people go against the prevailing wisdom and use a counterintuitive approach? But, you can be sure that sometimes, they … are … right.

It's what inspired American poet Robert Frost when he wrote "The Road Not Taken," where he considered two possible paths, one worn and the other nearly untrodden. Frost must have known something, as he was awarded four Pulitzer Prizes.

Here's an example of someone who did a lot of seemingly counterintuitive things. Let's protect his identity at least until you guess who it is. Let's call him Mr. X.

Lots of people lose money investing and starting companies. But Mr. X did it in a big way. He poured a lot of money, including his own, by investing and starting companies that were outside the norm of what were generally accepted viable business ideas, and he did this with three atypical companies at the same time. The businesses were so outside the norm of what everyone else was doing that experts in those industries often mocked his plans (maybe they secretly thought he was a donkey).

So, it wasn't a big surprise to the naysayers when countless delays and continued expenses sped the companies toward bankruptcy. Still, he kept pouring his money into them until it was gone. So, after one counterintuitive decision after another, he'd gone through his fortune, and even had to sell his car. About this time, his wife divorced him. He was repeatedly thrashed in the media.

So, there were lots of counterintuitive things that he did, including his take on the criticism. He was quoted as saying, "Always seek negative feedback, even though it can be mentally painful. They won't always be right, but I find the single biggest error people make is to ignore constructive, negative feedback."[38] Seeking negative feedback is certainly contrary to how most people feel.

In addition to (1) accepting criticism, here are other counterintuitive things I've observed that can actually be good practices.

1. Put yourself on the line.

    Basically, almost *nobody* wants to be the one stuck with the big problem—because when it goes wrong, they don't want to be anywhere near it. On October 2, 1945, a friend of President Harry Truman made and mailed him the sign that remained on his desk that said, "The BUCK STOPS here!" More than seventy years later, and it's still memorable because it's counterintuitive.

2. Intrinsic motivators are more important than extrinsic motivators.

    You might think what drives people is money or power, but studies conclusively show that the opportunity to collaborate, contribute, and make a difference are much bigger motivations.

3. **It's OK to be wrong.**
   It's been drilled into us our entire lives that the right answer gets the points on the tests or in the corporate world. But the hard reality is that if you're generally right all the time, you're generally not reaching far enough.

4. **It's OK to not know the answer.**
   Astrophysicist Neil deGrasse Tyson said, "It's okay not to know all the answers. It's better to admit our ignorance, than to believe answers that might be wrong. Pretending to know everything, closes the door to finding out what's really there."

5. **It's OK to be different.**
   Think about it: basically everyone who has accomplished a remarkable achievement is different. This isn't just about the mad genius artists, brilliant scientists, or revolutionary industrialists. The quiet, single parent who manages to successfully raise his or her children into productive, giving, and loving adults is also remarkable.

   My dad likes to tell the story (ahem, repeatedly) about how a nun from my school called him in for a "private meeting" one day, where he was asked by the sister about the "evident trouble at home." He had no idea what she was talking about, but the nun explained she could tell something was awry, as my little brother (probably in first grade at the time) had used red and purple to color the trees and skies in his coloring book. My parents moved us to a public school the following year.

   Forty some years later, my brother had a cabin in rural Alaska and painted it tangerine orange with red stripes. It looked cool as hell. Even the pilots flying overhead loved it. It was probably a message to Sister Thaddeus.

6. **Listen more (talk less).**
   It's hard to learn something new when you're talking. William Ury is the cofounder of Harvard's Program on Negotiation, author of seven books, and has consulted for dozens of Fortune 500 companies, and the White House. He's served as an advisor or mediator to corporate mergers, wildcat coalmine strikes, and countries struggling with

ethnic wars. In an excellent TED Talk, Ury explains when you listen to someone, they're more likely to listen to you.[39]

7. Remain a beginner/student.
    There's a great Zen quote, "In the beginner's mind there are many possibilities, in the expert's mind there are few." Maybe that's the simple reason so many amazing leaps are made by young minds—they didn't know it couldn't be done.

8. Unplug.
    Get away from the constant interruptions resulting from being online. Turn off the external interruptions. Tune in on your thinking.

9. Go with your gut.
    In an era when the business world is abuzz with metrics, data mining, analytics, etc., etc., sometimes you still have to simply trust your gut.

> *"There can be as much value in the blink of an eye as in months of rational analysis."*
> —Malcolm Gladwell

10. Sometimes bozos succeed.
    I've seen it. You've seen it.

11. Life is not fair.
    I've seen it. You've seen it.

12. Be real.
    Often the tendency is to want to not look the fool. To look cool. To fake it 'til you make it. But remember that those who mind don't matter, and those who matter don't mind.

So, back to our example extraordinaire of counterintuitive things—Mr. X. He persisted through the most difficult times, teetering for a time on financial ruin. Slowly, his companies started to gain traction and in 2018 Mr. X (Elon Musk) is CEO of SpaceX; CEO of Tesla, Inc.; CEO of Neuralink; founder of The Boring Company; and chairman of SolarCity. These companies are revolutionizing their respective industries.

"Two roads diverged ... I took the one less traveled by,
And that has made all the difference.
—Robert Frost

Career Advice from the World's Most Famous Robots

There's a lot of uncertainty about the future of American jobs. And it's understandable. The highly respected research firm Gartner published a report stating that 30 percent of the current jobs will be eliminated by 2025. And for those of us thinking that applies to jobs like tollbooth attendants, Gartner made a point of noting, "white collar jobs are certainly not immune."

So, yea ... people are nervous.

Robots, neural nets, machine learning, artificial intelligence, autonomous vehicles, package delivery drones, and the Internet of Things (IoT) are all working together with big data analytics to outperform whatever we might be doing for a living. And IoT means sensors embedded in everything (heck, probably even sensors inside other sensors).

I, for one, have good reason to be nervous. Harking way back to the earliest days when I bought a Mac in 1984, and personal computers were basically the equivalent of a four-month-old baby in diapers—I couldn't even beat the game "Chessmaster 2000"—on the easiest level, no less. The chess game had this highly advanced (cheesy robotic) speech emulator that would announce "checkmate" after its final move of every single game I played. It's a distant memory, but I recall the feeling of machine intelligence inexorably overtaking human capability. Actually, that's a wild exaggeration, but the Chessmaster 2000 did convey a tone of smugness each time it announced its win.

Looking at where technology is today, it's hard to predict how quickly this stuff is advancing. Today I bought a bottle of water from a vending machine, but out dropped a Coca-Cola. Was it a mistake? Or was a machine conspiring to shorten my life? So, where do we go to get answers on successfully navigating our futures within this rapidly evolving, new world? And what exactly are the odds of successfully competing alongside these smart androids?

Like you, I've learned from some smart people in my life—including parents, teachers, coworkers, and friends. After some deep thinking, it struck me like a bolt of lightning what they all had in common. They were all humans. Not wanting to limit myself to good ol' living sapiens, I went straight to the wisest sources I could find—robots.

Here are some lessons from the world's most famous robots on successfully navigating your future and the odds of doing so.

1. KITT: *Knight Rider*

> *"It is essential to your survival that you calm yourself and complete this task."*

Knight Industries Two Thousand (KITT) is giving two important lessons here, which will greatly contribute to you having a successful career: to keep cool and to complete your work.

That's good advice, especially from a talking car. And while keeping emotionally calm is easy for a robot, a lot of people find this to be a challenge at times. Yet, experience shows us that it's often difficult to make good rational decisions when emotions get the better of us. Keep your RPMs low.

2. Optimus Prime: *Transformers*

> *"Fate rarely calls upon us at a moment of our choosing."*

Take it from a robot that transforms from a semi-truck, Optimus Prime is correct. We have to be ready to seize our destiny when opportunity or challenge presents itself.

3. T-800: *Terminator*

> *"I'll be back!"*

Everyone is going to have their share of successes and failures. So commit right now to being tenacious and reliable in your pursuits. Repeat the words "I'll be back" as self-encouragement.

4. HAL 9000: *2001: A Space Odyssey*

> *"I am putting myself to the fullest possible use, which is all,*
> *I think, that any conscious entity can ever hope to do."*

The heuristically programmed algorithmic (HAL) system wasn't even really a robot, but more like a supercomputer that spied on everybody and ran the entire spaceship. At some point, HAL 9000 got a little big for his britches (computer talk) and started taking over control of the spaceship. But HAL, nonetheless, doled out some excellent wisdom in this quote. Basically, he's saying, "Be all you can be." Plus he's watching you and knows if you're trying hard enough.

5. RoboCop: *RoboCop*

> *"Serve the public trust, protect the innocent, uphold the law."*

Enough said!

6. Robot: *Lost in Space*

> *"He who chickens and runs away will chicken out another day."*

Be courageous! There will always be doubt and uncertainty. Be bold. Be confident. And those habits get strengthened with repeated use. Also, let me point out that this is the only rhyming text I found from any robot.

7. Bishop: *Aliens*

> *"Not bad for a ... human."*

Keep a sense of humor. Bishop was a loyal friend who kept his head, even when his head was severed by an alien attack.

8. Data: *Star Trek*

> *"In the event of a water landing, I have been*
> *designed to serve as a flotation device."*

Be adaptable. What's more, be willing to do some things below your capability at times. Data was a super-rational and intelligent robot, yet he was happy to act as a foam pool noodle, if necessary.

9. TARS: *Interstellar*

> *"Absolute honesty isn't always the most diplomatic nor the safest form of communication with emotional beings."*

How do I look? What do you think? Do you like the new recipe I tried? Sometimes a little care and kindness in responding goes a long way toward bolstering and supporting another person.

TARS isn't advocating lying and deception, but rather recognizing the value in maintaining civility and consideration for others.

10. C-3PO: *Star Wars*

> *"Sir, the possibility of successfully navigating an asteroid field is approximately 3,720 to 1."*

I wanted to better understand the odds of successfully navigating our futures within this rapidly unfolding new future world. And based on what C-3PO said about navigating an asteroid field—I decided to take the final lesson on probabilities from a human.

Replying to C-3PO, the inimitable Han Solo said, " Never tell me the odds."

Career Path or Ninja Warrior Course?

I'm going to give you some great career advice. Seriously, this probably should be communicated by whispering to you while hidden in a misty fog—so use your imagination. Here goes … When considering career choices, always consult a ninja warrior. You're welcome.

Jinichi Kawakami is the last ninja warrior and only heir to ninjutsu, which is the strategy and tactics used by ninja warriors. He's trained in just about everything you could imagine a ninja warrior would be, including swords, pyrotechnics, poisons, throwing weapons, hand-to-hand combat, horsemanship, and concealment. As far as I know, he might be watching me as I write this. Impossible to tell. Maybe he's somehow disguised himself as the chair I'm sitting on now.

So, what led me to learn from Kawakami? The answer is fear. I was invited to speak to a group of graduate students at Duke University's Fuqua School of Business on the topic of finding their paths. It was an invitation for which I felt like the wrong person.

The truth is, I couldn't have determined even my own career path. It's been decades of working in several different functional roles and within different industries. It includes Fortune 100 companies and small entrepreneurial startups. Aerospace, medical devices, software and IT services, giant hovercraft, and more. But, when it comes to the "path"? It's only in hindsight that I can see what led where.

The path has been continual change, learning, remaining flexible, being collaborative, and leading by example. And I'd be remiss if I didn't acknowledge the mistakes and the hard work along the way. I'm certainly not alone. The changing workplace over the past decades has a great many professionals continually tackling one challenging obstacle (project) after another.

It's basically the career equivalent of metaphorically running the course on the *American Ninja Warrior* television show. It's a course where participants jump, climb, lift, and balance their way through various (and changing) obstacles like the Salmon Ladder, the Warped Wall, the Cargo Net, and the Cannonball Drop.

The working world has us encountering the Clueless Boss Barrier, Insufficient Resource Reservoir, Quality Quicksand, and Interdepartmental Monkey Bars. That got me thinking about ninjas, and why I include the thoughts from Jinichi Kawakami, the last real ninja warrior.

Here are my ninja-influenced recommendations.

1. There is no one path.

   Your path can't be known in advance. Just like stealthily sneaking into a compound in the dark of night to rescue a princess (or competing on the *American Ninja Warrior* course) there will always be new obstacles. For one thing, the world is rapidly changing. Technology connects everyone, and makes the world a smaller place. There's massive knowledge sharing, and subsequently things change faster than ever.

   There's disagreement on the estimated number of "different careers" new graduates will have in their lifetimes. But regardless of whatever the number turns out to be, your career will be in flux.

2. Never stop learning.

   We all have many different jobs and meet many different people. The only element that is going to be a constant in each of those situations and projects is each one of us. The way you add more value is by bringing more to the engagement. What will you bring?

   The great news is that there are innumerable sources from which you can continue your education. First, there's the workplace itself, along with those you'll work alongside. There are books, online and offline courses, Toastmasters for speaking, and Meetup groups for everything.

3. Never stop training.

   The strongest professional I ever met never stopped practicing to get better. Steve Jobs, who you might think could just show up and rock a product presentation, would practice not for hours … but for days, constantly rehearsing, editing, and refining. Are you better than that?

Even competitors on *American Ninja Warrior* replicate the obstacle courses in their backyards, basements, or garages, and then train for years. That's what it takes to get better.

How long until you're superhuman and can run across a pond or disappear in a blink? "That is impossible because no matter how much you train, ninjas were people," laughs Kawakami.

4. Nobody cares about your goals.
   You're on your own. That's a hard truth. And this relates to the importance of the prior advice of continuous learning and training. Yes, a new job will have its initial share of welcoming enthusiasm and interest. But that will quickly dissipate in the wind. The good news (actually the great news) is that you are responsible for your own happiness and goals. Not a parent, or a spouse, or a boss. It's all you, ninja baby.

5. Be selfless.
   Approach your job with the questions, "What can I contribute? Who can I help?" Even the competitors on *American Ninja Warrior* are all cheering for one another. They realize their only real competition is with themselves. As in the working world, there is no limit to the number of people who could conquer the course.

6. Pay attention to the why.
   Every leader (or ninja warrior) has a "why." It's the essence of why they do what they do. For Bono, the lead singer of U2, it's to make meaningful music and better the world, which led him to persuade global leaders to write-off debt owed by impoverished countries and to enlist companies and millions of people in the fight against AIDS. Bono is probably a ninja.

   When describing the origination of ninjas in ancient Japan, Kawakami explains the ninjas were committed to bettering the community. The harmony of all the residents in the village as a whole, became more important than individual needs. A true ninja tries to create harmony in the community.

7. Be collaborative.
   Great work happens when people come together, cooperate, and

collaborate. According to Kawakami, Japanese people developed the ability to hide their feelings and learned to read other people and act accordingly.

8. Graduating is the beginning.
    You know this already.

And here's the opportunity for you. Despite having many students, Kawakami has decided he will not appoint anyone as the next ninja grandmaster. Kawakami now spends much of his time teaching ninja history part-time at Mie University.

So, there's no sense in waiting to be appointed. Go become a ninja warrior. That was said to you like a whisper from beyond the tall grass. And … poof … I've vanished!

Half Your New Goals Will Fail (If You're a Badass)

My first manager was a badass, and he was the smartest person I'd ever met. Bill Briggs was so much smarter than me, that it took me decades (of life and work), to realize that the one thing he said—that seemed obviously wrong at the time—was actually obviously right.

Bill grew up in northern California, had a master's degree from the Massachusetts Institute of Technology (MIT) and a beard with a little gray that added to him being a cool, laid-back, brilliant guy. He was always in a good mood. He hired me as a new engineer straight out of Purdue University, and I eagerly moved to join him at a large technology company in California. We designed and built advanced equipment used by US Navy ships, planes, and submarines.

One day, we were talking in his office about effort and success. It was probably about a new project at work, but Bill's answer was intended generally. To this day, I remember exactly what he said. "I try to always get things right," Bill said, "but on average, if I can get just more than about half of my new things to work out—that's good." Bill was kind of laughing when he said it, but he wasn't joking.

I was dumbstruck. This guy was the smartest person I knew, and he said nearly half his endeavors didn't work out as planned? What the hell! I thought he was going to say, "maybe 1 or 2 percent of the time he was wrong." I stood there looking at him. Bill took out a stick of gum from his desk and offered it to me. It was Juicy Fruit.

Here's what I've learned over the decades since then.

Let's say you work to develop a product that utilizes some emerging technology,

or you launch a new service into the market,

or you start a new venture,

or you strive to set a personal best time for a 5K run,

or you write an article that resonates with people,

or whatever.

If, on average, you can get more than half of your stuff to work out—that's exceptionally good. Seriously, you are a rock star of getting new stuff to work out.

Here's a billion-dollar example of someone who got only *one-third* of his new stuff to succeed. Turns out it's someone else named Bill, and it involves the gum my manager gave me that day.

Bill Wrigley arrived in Chicago in 1891 with only $32. His idea was to start a business selling scouring soap. Sales of his soap were slow, so he did what many marketers do and tried to entice customers by including something else—in this case a small can of baking powder. It turned out Wrigley's baking powder was more popular with customers—so he switched his business to selling baking powder.

Then to encourage his customers to buy more baking powder, he decided to include some chewing gum. And this time, he learned his chewing gum was more popular with customers than the baking powder. So Wrigley switched businesses again—this time to selling gum.

Switching from scouring soap to baking powder and finally to gum was Wrigley's third pivot to a new business. Even a success ratio of 33 percent can result in world-class achievement. By comparison, approximately 85 percent of new consumer packaged goods (CPG) products fail within two years.

Fast-forward to 2008, when the Mars company acquired the Wm. Wrigley Jr. Company for $23 billion. That's a lot of Juicy Fruit, and from another badass named Bill.

Reverse Undercover Boss

Here's a scenario involving you. But it'll never happen. The CEO of your company gets picked to be on the television show *Undercover Boss* and is disguised as a new employee in your company. You are one of the few people who are selected to mentor and train this "new employee." All this, including your amazing abilities and underappreciated insights, are filmed for television broadcast.

Undercover Boss was first shown in the US in 2010. It has been produced in localized versions in 14 different countries with additional countries planned.

Here's what happens in each episode. A CEO or senior-level manager of a large company goes undercover, disguised as a new employee, and works at various jobs within the company—by being paired with another employee. It's a way for the undercover individual to surreptitiously learn about aspects of the company that he or she might not otherwise experience, and to get to know a few (typically) hardworking and underrepresented employees.

Once the individuals have completed their time undercover, they head back to their corner offices, whereupon the employees they worked with are called in for a meeting. "Do I look familiar?" The deserving (and shocked) employees, struggling with work and life issues, are typically awarded generous financial and training bonuses, and sincerely thanked for their efforts in making the company work. Of course, as with any of the "reality" shows on television, there's certainly a lot of "setup." But there's no denying, it's a learning experience.

In my imagined scenario, where the CEO is working in a new role with you, she or he is a bumbling but well-intended fool. What's more, you point out problems, difficulties, and real frustrations in the company that the leaders were clueless about. And beyond the CEO, you impress the heck out of everyone in America watching the show. So thanks for your patience and education! Truth is … you humble the CEO, and you play a real role in making the company work.

Mostly though, the CEO learns about you—that you care about the work, that you have worries and struggles and issues like everyone else. In fact, the CEO is actually a lot like you. Actually, everyone watching the episode is a lot like you. Which is why, in this scenario … after you're surprised to learn the "new employee" is actually the CEO ("I thought that long hair looked kind of weird!") you're awarded a sizable sum of money and are chosen to run a new company-wide initiative to identify a multitude of problem areas for improvement.

Unfortunately, as was said at the outset, that scenario will never happen. The CEO of your company is not selecting a wig to spend a few days under your tutelage (though if they were, you'd certainly get the previously mentioned awards). But the good news is you don't need to wait for the CEO to come to you disguised as a new employee. Here's a better suggestion that could actually show some benefits.

Flip it. You put together your own new look as the CEO—and approach your job with a new CEO-like perspective. The disguise or "new look" doesn't need to be with clothes, though you could try to look more of the part—whatever that means in your company. Mostly though, the "new look" is the perspective and the questions you bring to your work.

- What are the things about your job that need fixing?

- Why is the department doing things this way?

- How could these projects go smoother?

- What are all the things you're responsible for, and which ones matter the most?

- What things could you do differently, even as an experiment just a few times, to see if there are any improvements?

- What *extra* things could you do that would improve the quality of the work?

- How might the job change in three to five years, and what could you do to begin the changes?

- How could your eight hours of work get done in seven hours (or less)?

- What could you do outside your job? (Perhaps write a blog post, read a list of relevant books, meetup with people in similar jobs to compare and consider best practices, or interview industry thought leaders.)

- What could you analyze, test, or trial? Can you write a report of recommendations?

Doing those things will have you thinking and acting more like the improvement-seeking solution-searching person you are.

You'll be thinking beyond your normal day-to-day activities. Maybe you can add some colleagues. It might even be fun.

But the reality is … Your quest for improvements will probably be frustrating. It'll definitely require extra effort, working through lunches, and some late nights. You might be viewed with odd looks or even criticism from your colleagues. Some of your ideas will probably be lame. Many of your suggestions will be ignored. It won't be easy. And in the end, your work might not have any impact.

But regardless of the outcomes, you'll be better for the effort. You've stepped up and attempted to make things better. To improve the company and yourself. You'll begin to recognize yourself as a CEO, at least of the work and the people for which you're responsible. Soon others will recognize you too. That's something you can't disguise.

The Secret to Great Work

The refrigerator was dangling precariously from a rope about 20 feet in the air. Definitely not where it should be. I watched it break free and fall … on top of two guys working below. There was a massive crash and a lot of commotion. I don't remember what happened next. But I do know both guys were fine. It was the magicians and illusionists Penn and Teller, who were performing their show in Los Angeles, aptly titled "The Refrigerator Tour."

I know enough about magic to know that a magician *never* reveals the secret. But this is something I've thought a lot about, so the rule will be broken. For one thing, I'm not a magician. For another, the secret could be applied to your business or line of work. The third rationalization for giving it away, is that I heard Penn Jillette talking about the magic and he let out the secret (perhaps inadvertently) during an excellent interview with James Altucher.[40]

Should I be afraid?

Penn Jillette is six foot seven inches tall and is the boisterous ringmaster for the duo, while Teller basically never speaks on stage (he learned while performing in college that if he said nothing, he was less likely to have hecklers throw things at him). My point is that Jillette could hurt me, and Teller ain't talkin'. Besides, it's fairly apparent they could certainly make me disappear.

They're bright, talented, and hard-working—and have come a long way since they started performing in the 1970s, when they were basically living out of their car and working nonstop. They have been headlining at the Rio in Las Vegas since 2001, have their own television show, and were recently awarded a star on the Hollywood Walk of Fame (near the star dedicated to Houdini).

"Doing beautiful things is its own reward."
—Teller

So, what's their secret. Here goes ...

Penn (I'm using his first name as a technique to get friendly before spilling the beans) explains their general thinking in these sentences cleverly hidden throughout the interview.

"What I've learned, in art, you need both inspiration and skills."

"Once you get the brilliant idea, then you have to do the massive hard work."

"The most important thing is everything."

"You've got to be brave enough to do shit that is absolutely buck-nutty crazy, and then you've got to work hard enough to make that being done perfectly skillful."

Then my friend, Penn, who I greatly respect (ahem) explains what *really* goes on behind the curtain!

"There is only one trick we do. And that trick is we're willing to work harder than you think we would work. We just put in a trick in the show that runs three minutes, that Teller and I worked on for six years solid. You would not work six years to do three minutes. We would."

Dear Penn and Teller, Don't hurt me. It was a secret that needed to be told.

Survival Lessons from the First Fish in Space

I'm not above taking advice from a fish. Especially the first fish in space. The questions scientists and NASA wanted to know was, "How would a fish swim in a completely new environment of zero gravity? How would a fish (or a school of fish) orient itself?"

If you think about it, it's a great question! There is no "up" or "down" in zero gravity. In fact, if you're swimming while in space, there's not even a "sideways" or a "crooked." There's no gravity for the fish to orient itself. So NASA took live fish up to space and let them swim around in zero gravity. What they found out was really interesting.

There were two main lessons I caught from this study. So, thank you, NASA and scientists, and my apologies to the fish for using the word caught. I think the surprising findings will help guide my future!

Aside from being an interesting question to any curious person, it got me thinking about applying the findings here on Earth. Even with gravity, things can feel a bit disorienting in our careers and lives. Sometimes it seems the world is changing so fast, that the old "right-side-up" rules don't quite apply.

A study by Oxford University said 47 percent of the current jobs will disappear in the next 25 years, largely due to robots, automation, and artificial intelligence.[41]

Historically, technology displaced jobs, but those losses were offset by the creation of new jobs required to support the new technologies. Such was the case with the Industrial Revolution, when machines and factories resulted in the significant elimination of many craftspeople. Although a large percentage of those folks then retrained and went to work in those factories building, operating, and repairing the machines.

But researchers say the coming revolution is different, as a large number of displaced jobs are not going to be replaced in other areas of employment. As is always the case, there's some disagreement among the economists and academics who study such things. Predicting the future is slippery business, and not as simple as shooting fish in a barrel. I couldn't resist using two fish metaphors in one sentence. Take time to mullet over.

But, regardless of the specifics, there's going to be major disruption and subsequent disorientation resulting from the accelerating impact of technologies including driverless vehicles, artificial intelligence (AI), automation, etc.

So, here are two lessons from the fish when they experienced zero gravity environment in space.

1. Keep moving.

   When faced with a new (weightless) environment, the fish kept moving like they were swimming around in the bay down on Earth. This, of course, was necessary, as the water moving through their gills provided them oxygen to live.

   Maybe this isn't too surprising. But, on the other hand, maybe if we were in space we'd just float around, stare out the window, eat freeze-dried astronaut ice cream, and stop exercising. Hopefully, we'll all keep moving when our environment changes.

   "Intelligence is the ability to adapt to change."
   —Stephen Hawking

2. Move toward the light.

   For the first few days in their zero gravity environment, the fish swam in random, directional ovals. There was no gravity pulling them to indicate which way was up or which way was down. Without directional orientation, they swam in upside-down and sideways loops. However, after a few days, the fish eventually settled on what was consistently their "up" and "down!"

   How did they do that? Wherever the light originated, the fish assumed that to be "up." After all, the sunlight is always shining from above when they're on Earth. So, eventually the fish always kept their backs to the interior lighting within the space lab. That makes sense. Even the fish learned to orient themselves to the light.

"Fear is the path to the dark side. Fear leads to anger. Anger leads to hate. Hate leads to suffering."
—Yoda

So thank you to the fish for teaching me those two vital lessons on adapting to change. Keep moving and orient using the light. You don't have to be a brain sturgeon to keep their pioneering spaceflight in mind as we navigate the changing world here on Earth.

If you think of a better fish pun ... let minnow.

"No good fish goes anywhere without a porpoise."
—Lewis Carroll

Lessons from Working with Leaders

There's nothing quite like working with great people. During a recent business trip, I thought about the things I've learned from some of the great people with whom I've had the pleasure of working. I simply thought about those folks who've made lasting positive impressions, those I learned from and wanted to imitate. It goes without saying—you don't need to be the person at the top to lead. So, certainly, these lessons were learned from folks at all levels.

The list flowed readily within just a few minutes. In no particular order, other than the order in which these lessons came to mind, here is what I noted.

- Be candid, be direct, and be considerate.

- Let your word be your bond.

- Show up early, everywhere.

- Take time for lunch.

- Pitch in and do whatever needs to be done. Don't wait for an invitation, and don't wait for somebody else to get started first. It's ok to be the first. Others will follow you (or not).

- Go home at night and get your rest.

- Set aggressive goals and drive yourself (and those you're leading) to attain them. People want to pursue big goals.

- Insist on a written schedule and plan. A verbal plan is not worth the paper it's not printed on.

- Work weekends, evenings, and early morning when needed.

- Start your day early.

- Don't worry about the things you can't control.

- Be nice. That doesn't mean you can't be direct and hold people accountable.

- Politely acknowledge the naysayers and doubters who offer no constructive criticism, then promptly discard their opinions and move along steadfastly with your efforts.

- Be generous with your time.

- Structure business dealings where all the parties have a shared interest in the same outcome.

- Be a gentleman or a lady. Being polite, considerate, and exhibiting some class are distinct characteristics that always reflect positively.

- Be steadfast.

- Never make a threat.

- Trust your instincts. They're coming from the most advanced-thinking machine in the known universe—the human brain.

- Take responsibility for your own career and life. Outside of your children or your spouse … nobody really cares.

- Make the hard decisions.

- Stay physically active. Our bodies were made to move. Move. Every day.

- Adapt to change, including new technologies. Usually things are awkward and slow going at first. Get used to it. Learn. Improve. Repeat.

- Try new things.

- Don't be afraid.

- Dress like a professional.

- Swear infrequently.

- Control your temper and remain collected.

- Set your sites on the future, and really make a point of enjoying the day—today.

What You Learn from a Difficult (Career) Path

This is embarrassing to admit, but when I was in first grade, my mom got me a little briefcase. This had nothing to do with my wanting to be a businessman, but it had everything to do with my wanting to be James Bond. She even wrote on the inside in block lettering, "Property of 007." It was the only attaché case in the entire St. Joseph Catholic school. No surprise.

While waiting for the bus at the end of the day, one of the older kids purposely kicked my briefcase across the paved parking lot. I remember watching it slide like a big, black, hockey puck.

I loved James Bond. He was tough and cool. He defeated lots of bad guys, and by the end of the movie, he saved the world. Bond would overcome ridiculous odds through cleverness, confidence, tenacity, and well-honed skills.

And like most boys, I loved gadgets. And Bond had lots of innovative technology—a rocket belt, an underwater jet pack, a mini rocket cigarette, and a Rolex with a rotating bezel that cuts ropes (and let him escape from a tank of man-eating sharks). But maybe all that toughness and all those inventions pale in comparison to the tenacity required to create the man himself.

Before he became 007, James Bond was homeless. Well, more accurately, the actor Daniel Craig was homeless. Craig was a struggling actor with no money, and he slept on park benches. It should have been obvious that villains in the movie wouldn't stand a chance against him. The guy slept on park benches for a time.

And if James Bond is not your cup of tea (the British reference was unavoidable), there are a shocking number of other successful people who were also homeless at one time. They include Suze Orman, Jim Carrey, Ella Fitzgerald, Houdini, Sylvester Stallone, and Charlie Chaplin—to name just several.

I can't imagine the difficulty and hardship involved in moving from the streets to establishing a successful career and life. But, amazingly, some people do it. Perhaps not surprisingly, they credit their early struggles with helping build the framework for their future successes.

Here is what some people have said that being homeless taught them.

1. Innovation

   It probably goes without saying, but creativity and invention are often necessary in creating a new future to move toward. Without that invented or imagined destiny, you'd have no goal and would stop making progress.

   John Paul DeJoria, the founder of the hair-care company John Paul Mitchell Systems and an American billionaire says, "When you start with next to nothing, all you've got is a lot of thought, a lot of innovation, figuring new ways to do things without using a lot of money." He was homeless twice.

2. Courage.

   The fear of being stuck, of failing, must feel incredibly discouraging. And that fear needs to be pushed aside with bravery.

   Turns out David Letterman spent time living in his red 1973 Chevy pickup while he was a struggling comedian in Los Angeles. Dave said, "There's only one requirement of any of us, and that is to be courageous. Because courage, as you might know, defines all other human behavior. And, I believe—because I've done a little of this myself—pretending to be courageous is just as good as the real thing."

3. A Sense of Humor

   It's hard to imagine maintaining a sense of humor about such a difficult situation. But Joan Rivers, the Emmy-winning television show host and comedienne, spent some time living in her car, said it was critical. "Life goes by fast. Enjoy it. Calm down. It's all funny. Next. Everyone gets so upset about the wrong things."

4. Taking Action

   No doubt, the ability to continue putting one foot in front of the other and moving toward your goal is essential in making progress. Whoever told you "Nothing comes to those who wait" was right.

Tyler Perry, the actor, director, writer, producer, and playwright, lived in his Geo Metro convertible in the mid-1990s. His words of advice, "The key to life when it gets tough is to keep moving. Just keep moving."

5. Empathy
Although nobody wants to endure hardship for long, it does provide perspective. In general, and whether you believe it or not, there's often a thin line and a small number of events that separates people and their seemingly wildly different situations.

Singer-songwriter and musician Ed Sheeran, who at times slept on the Central Line and outside Buckingham Palace said, "Be nice to everyone, always smile, and appreciate things because it could all be gone tomorrow."

6. Persistence
Actress Halle Berry slept in a homeless shelter in New York City for a time. "There have been so many people who have said to me, 'You can't do that,' but I've had an innate belief that they were wrong. Be unwavering and relentless in your approach."

7. Belief
Like a lot of things in life, what people do depends on what they believe they can do.

Jean-Claude Van Damme slept on the streets of Los Angeles, working for his break in Hollywood. "I came to America with a dream and I made it. The dream became reality. America is built for success."

I continued taking my 007 briefcase to first grade, but as I continued through school, I found an even better character to imitate—Captain Kirk, the commander of the *USS Enterprise*. He was cool under pressure, utilized lots of innovations (he went into warp drive in every show, for goodness sake), and was a good leader. Captain Kirk also had to deal with things not even James Bond encountered—aliens. In hindsight, it should have been obvious that aliens wouldn't stood a chance against Captain Kirk. Turns out, William Shatner also spent some time nearly broke and living in his pickup truck.

A Hypercompetitive World: Globalization and Technology

The Disruptive Impact of Globalization and Technology

Take a look at the changes happening within essentially any industry today, and it's obvious how quickly the pace of change is accelerating. New innovations and new products are being brought to market with such increasing frequency that the acceleration of change can seem a bit daunting.

We hardly need any evidence of our rapidly changing world. After all, we're inundated daily with ads for new products and media stories of the next big thing. But to gain a little perspective on the increase in innovation and change, think back just two or three decades about a couple of everyday examples with which we're all familiar—groceries and automobiles.

Cleaning Up in Aisle Six

Everyone has some firsthand market and product experience. My parents had a small grocery and meat store, and as someone who stocked the shelves year after year, I can tell you that there were relatively few new product introductions. The big news was the cola wars and the Pepsi Challenge of Pepsi vs. Coke, which was a genius move by a brilliant marketer and business leader—John Sculley. But the ingredients were unchanged. As far as innovative new products, there was not a lot happening.

Today it's a different story. It seems there is a constant influx of new grocery products fighting for attention. And often there are entirely new categories emerging and changing the product landscape. Take energy drinks as one example. To get an idea as to the rate of growth, Red Bull was created in Austria in 1987 and launched in the US in 1997. The energy drink category grew to approximately $43 billion worldwide in 2016.[42] Wikipedia lists 60 different energy drink brands (Red Bull, Rockstar, Monster, and 5-hour Energy are the popular ones), and there's probably several more launching by the time I finish this sentence.

Zero to Sixty in 60 kWh

Another example of an industry undergoing rapid change is the automotive industry. Before the influx of Japanese automobiles, the cars coming out of Detroit, Michigan, really didn't change that much from year to year. There just wasn't an environment of fierce competition to drive consistent and significant innovation.

But consider what began with the introduction of Japanese automobiles into the US, and what continues today within the automotive industry. Cars are continually being released with significant mechanical and electrical advances. Even a partial listing of automotive features being added now or in the near future reads like a dream list from *Popular Mechanics:* rear-mounted radar, night vision with pedestrian detection, automatic high beam control (unlike old controls that switched from high to low beam, this technology actually gradually increases or decreases the light pattern), parental control (to limit speed), GPS vehicle tracking (watch your car live on the internet), built-in cameras, internet for passengers, etc.

And that doesn't even mention self-parking, self-driving, hybrid, or fully electric cars like Tesla Motors—which promise major changes beyond the innovative automobile itself—including fueling stations, recycling batteries, cleaner emissions, etc.

Two things are clear to me, more innovation is occurring faster than ever before, and the global business world has undergone profound changes. But what are the reasons behind these fundamental shifts?

Global Business Strategist Richard D'Aveni

To further understand what is driving all this innovation and change within the world of business, I had the privilege of speaking with Richard D'Aveni of the Tuck School of Business at Dartmouth. D'Aveni is one of the world's preeminent strategists who has worked for three decades with multinational corporations and major governments throughout the world to assist with their strategies.[43]

As evident from his several books on the topic and his enthusiasm, Professor D'Aveni is passionate about understanding the seismic changes happening and in communicating new strategies for success. He explains the corporate strategies, that companies used for decades, have been under attack as a result of globalization and technology. According to D'Aveni, the old corporate strategic theories, along with the old business models are falling apart. The resulting impact on businesses has ranged from creating a challenging business environment (automobiles, consumer electronics) all the way to creating major industry upheavals (music, newspapers).

Traditional Business Strategies

Historically, the first rule of business strategy that corporations used was to find and leverage a sustainable competitive advantage. Perhaps the company had access to a geographically concentrated pool of factory workers or engineers. Or it had the critical mass to have its own fleet of vehicles for product distribution, had a secret manufacturing technique, or was geographically situated in a location that had a unique advantage. Such sustainable competitive advantages were often the reason a customer would pick a company over its competitor.

But in today's global business environment, and with technology that connects everyone at the speed of light, many competitive advantages have greatly diminished or even been eliminated. Access to engineers and scientists is now readily available anywhere there is internet, UPS will handle distribution and logistics for a multitude of small- and medium-size businesses, world-class cloud software is affordable and readily available to even a one-person company, and a small business can reach customers around the world for next to nothing.

Another primary business strategy used during the 20th century was for companies to use their strengths against a competitor's weakness. Typically, this strategy was ascertained by the business development and marketing folks completing a SWOT analysis—where the company would describe its strengths, weaknesses, opportunities, and threats. Then the managers, with their SWOT analysis in hand, would begin planning and executing how best to deploy their strengths against a competitor's weaknesses.

But D'Aveni points out that many new disruptive technologies and business models now force firms to build their weaknesses and to overwhelm the strengths of rivals. The old SWOT rule of leveraging your core competence is now a way to milk your firm's current assets. Instead, firms should be preparing for the future by turning weaknesses into new competitive advantages that shift the rules of the game.

Managers have been taught the above strategies for decades, and those strategies are still being taught today in many institutions. According to D'Aveni, who has researched and written about this topic in several books, continuing with these primary strategies has been a mistake for which businesses pay dearly.

Traditional Strategies No Longer Work

Professor D'Aveni explains in his books, classroom, and consulting engagements with companies, that those long-held traditional strategies were premised on a slower change of pace and lower levels of disruption. While they were viable strategies decades ago, he has shown how globalization and technology (and to an extent regulation) have long negated those practices. He wrote about this new environment in his book *Hypercompetition: Managing the Dynamics of Strategic Maneuvering*, and coined the term. These concepts of temporary competitive advantage and hypercompetition were first written by D'Aveni in 1994, and since that time, there have been many imitators, followers, and adopters of his ideas.

What D'Aveni explains is that the old rules are being destroyed as a result of a global shift in business competition caused by globalization and technology. This fundamental shift, results in a world where finding a "sustainable competitive advantage" is no longer viable. Where using your strengths against a competitor's weakness will eventually lead to failure. As an explanation, Professor D'Aveni describes a general history arc of the automotive industry over the past 100 years, which he adds is similar to many other industries during the same period.

A Brief History of How We Got Where We Are

When the automobile industry began, there were tremendous innovations related to engine performance, braking, and suspension systems. There were also major innovations concerning manufacturing and production assembly. Henry Ford, founder of the Ford Motor Company, was a champion of the assembly line. Eventually, as the industry matured and a few key competitors emerged, the industry evolved into a small oligopoly, and the innovations lessened. The model was not to drive the other competitor out of business, but more or less to divide the market.

The market changed to one where there was "planned obsolescence" of the products. Many executives considered this a great management practice. It allowed car companies to overcharge and make good profit, while producing mediocre products. D'Aveni describes the result as one where the manufacturers treated the customers and suppliers poorly, while treating the competition well. He points out that this is something that seems backward today.

But the unwritten rules were within the US, and foreign competitors had different rules of competition. Previously, the automotive industry could discredit a cutthroat attitude. But Japan entered the market and it didn't care about US rules. The Japanese vehicles were of high quality, reliable, and affordable. Over the ensuing years, Detroit and the US auto industry was decimated.

As further evidence of the changing world and strategies, D'Aveni mentioned a couple of hugely popular business books: *Built to Last: Successful Habits of Visionary Companies*, by Jim Collins and Jerry Porras; and *In Search of Excellence: Lessons from America's Best-Run Companies*, by Thomas Peters and Robert Waterman. According to D'Aveni, these books profiled companies that were at the top of their industries for over 50 years. However, today only about one third of the companies have continued to earn money for shareholders at about their same historic rates. D'Aveni mentions that "Historical performance didn't predict the future." And that's the point D'Aveni has been trying to make for decades. "The old rules don't apply. The old rules have contributed to creating the weakest economy in decades."

The New Hypercompetitive World: Good News and Bad News

The historic strategies of the 20th century were about the ability to sustain leadership position by putting up barriers to entry and competing systematically with the competition. This was done in hundreds of industry sectors and by thousands of companies and was primarily accomplished by these methods.

1. Finding a sustainable competitive advantage, such as superior resources.

2. Conducting a SWOT analysis and using your strengths where the competitors were weak. (This is also typically used historically as a military strategy.)

But, technology and globalization have leveled the playing field and allowed new players to come into virtually every market, creating a world of hypercompetition where the old strategies are no longer effective.

The good news is that on the whole people benefit. The bad news is that competition is escalating. Competition is becoming increasingly fierce. There has been major disruption in numerous industries, and some industries have experienced such upheaval that they have had to deploy completely new business models.

So, exactly why don't the old strategies work any longer? In a word, because of hypercompetition, as Richard D'Aveni explains by use of an analogy.

Sustainable Competitive Advantage Is No Longer a Viable Strategy

As a simple means of describing to a large group of business executives why and how business strategy needs to evolve as a result of the new hypercompetitive world, Richard D'Aveni uses a simple thought experiment involving a tennis match.

He describes a hypothetical scenario in which two competing tennis players are equally matched. For the sake of example, he wants you to assume they're of identical skills and fitness levels; and that they both have strong forearms (same competitive advantage) and similarly weaker backhands. They're perfectly matched competitors, and, being equal, would each win an equal number of games.

Traditional Strategy

The only difference D'Aveni inserts into the above scenario, is that competitor "A" was taught the basic strategy of using a strength against an opponent's weakness—as per traditional business SWOT analysis. So, putting that strategy into practice, player A would use her forearm to hit the ball to player B's backhand whenever possible. Using that strategy, we could correctly assume that player A would win the first game in this matchup. Furthermore, player A would probably win the next several matches using the same strategy.

But, D'Aveni explains that because we're now competing in a hypercompetitive world with new rules, competitive landscape, and a greater number of "games played"—that consistently applying the old business strategy no longer works—at least not for long.

As an example of how the world has changed, he mentions Sony and Panasonic. "In the consumer electronics industry, product lifecycles used to be five years, now new products are introduced in five months. And while in the 1980s each company had a few thousand products, today they have between 60,000 and 70,000 products." So concerning the analogy of the tennis match, one game, or even a dozen games, doesn't reflect the real world today. A more apt analogy would be competing hundreds of times, perhaps on different courses with evolving rules.

Going back to the tennis scenario, after 100 games … player A has likely still won more games. But at this point, player B's backhand has gotten much better due to all the usage. In fact, D'Aveni argues that player B has likely by now probably developed her backhand into a second competitive advantage—in that her backhand is now better than player A's backhand. And that, he points out, is one of the problems in today's world when companies focus primarily on "leveraging their core competency." It's a formula for victory in the short term, but in this new world, it will likely lead to defeat in the long term. Focusing on using strengths often defocuses companies from developing their weaknesses. Yet old business habits are hard to break, and D'Aveni's lament is that business theory has become religion in the face of new world facts. "People are taking old rules and continuing to apply them without adaptation to a new world," D'Aveni says.

More Competition Requires New Strategy

Returning to his thought experiment, D'Aveni asks the business execs, "Now, if you were player B, after the first 100 matches what would you do during the next 100 games?" He gets good participation from the group, "Mix it up," "Run player A around," and "Continually change the pace." The professor smiles and nods his head positively. D'Aveni explains, "Exactly! If you were player B, rather than simply use your competitive advantages against the competition, which would be using your forehand and now your backhand to hit to player A's backhand, you'd change things up and be unpredictable."

This is the point D'Aveni has wanted to make, and indeed has been espousing for decades. He makes a point that historically, business strategy was to be clear and permanent, but in today's dynamic and ever-evolving world, it should be flexible.

Increased Competition Requires a Multitude of Varying Strategies

D'Aveni explains this scenario is what has similarly happened within numerous industries over the past 30 years in the United States. He asks the audience of senior business executives for their general thoughts on the discussion and the hypothetical tennis match. Their responses include the following ideas.

- The rules of competition have changed significantly over the past few decades.

- Rote focus on the traditional strategy of "using your strength against an opponent's weakness" will eventually lead to trouble.

- Through repeated usage, player B's weakness becomes a strength. Player B now has essentially two competitive advantages.

- Player A should have developed her weakness, rather than solely focus on using her strength against player B's weakness.

- In an environment of rapid change, a better long-term strategy would be to play unpredictably and "mix things up."

- Timing and speed of maneuvering become increasingly important.

- Once unpredictability and constant change is happening, the fierceness of competition goes way up.

- Unpredictability and constant change equate to competing and winning with temporary advantages.

The old business strategies involving finding a competitive advantage and attacking your opponent's weakness with your strengths are no longer effective in today's world. Rather, competing strategically by establishing dynamic temporary competitive advantages is increasingly required to establish and maintain business success.

In with the New, Out with the Old

The business world used to be different. Business strategy in the 20th century focused on the rules codified by Harvard Business School professor Michael Porter: slow-down the competition by finding a sustainable competitive advantage, establish oligopolies by creating barriers to entry, reduce rivalry through avoiding price competition, and attacking a competitor's weaknesses. Then use this noncompetitive environment to maximize margins by taking advantage of consumers through higher prices and lower quality. One other important rule codified by Porter was that firms should only offer higher quality for a higher price, or low quality for a low price, because this prevents margins from eroding.

Business schools in the 20th century taught generations of managers that this was considered fair competition, ignoring the detrimental effects of noncompetitive oligopolies and planned obsolescence. This was the thinking, Richard D'Aveni explains, which led the US automotive companies to essentially offer higher-priced, low-quality cars, and to open the doors for Japanese competitors to take market share by offering high quality and low prices at the same time. The major manufacturers made money, and lots of it, by acting as an oligopoly with power over customers and suppliers.

However, this environment didn't foster innovation, with a notable exception being the Tucker Corporation in the late 1940s, which developed many automotive innovations. The innovative Tucker car called for a rear engine; a low-RPM, 589-cubic inch engine with hydraulic valves instead of a camshaft, fuel-injection, direct-drive torque converters on each rear wheel (instead of a transmission); disc brakes; the location of all instruments within the diameter and reach of the steering wheel; a padded dashboard; self-sealing tubeless tires; independent, springless suspension; a chassis that protected occupants in a side impact; a roll bar within the roof; a laminated windshield designed to pop out during an accident; and a center "cyclops" headlight, which would turn when steering at angles greater than 10 degrees to improve visibility around corners during night driving.

Unfortunately, the Securities and Exchange Commission (SEC) investigated Tucker Corporation amid concerns about investments. Although the jury reached a verdict of "not guilty" on all counts for all accused, by the time the investigation and the trial were completed, the Tucker Corporation—without a factory, buried in debt, and faced with numerous lawsuits from Tucker dealers angry about the production delays—was no more. Perhaps you've seen the movie, *Tucker: The Man and His Dream* starring Jeff Bridges. (As an aside, the US attorney named Otto Kerner Jr., who had aggressively pursued the Tucker Corporation, was later convicted on 17 counts of bribery, conspiracy, perjury, and related charges for stock fraud in 1974. He was the first federal appellate judge in history to be jailed.)

In any event, the oligopoly continued until the foreign automakers entered the US and global market with a new competitive (zero-sum) attitude. They came to conquer and they acted as disrupters. The old business models might have assumed reasonably fair competition, but the new competition didn't play by the old rules. The US auto industry was vulnerable with poor products and a lack of innovations. Furthermore, the US product quality was weak. The onslaught of aggressive competition resulted in a drop in sales that shook the foundations of the US auto industry for decades.

It was a difficult period for Detroit, but after decades of turmoil and improvements, the US automobile manufacturers are once again building vehicles with world-class product innovation and quality.

The Cutting Edge of Innovation

It's not just cars and trucks that are operating within a continually changing market. Even something as seemingly staid as razor blades have experienced continuous innovation over the past 20 years. Gillette pours massive amounts of time and money into product research and development (R&D), and its frequent new product launches are major campaigns involving hundreds of millions of dollars.

As soon as a competitor is about to introduce a new product, Gillette introduces something better. Each shaving system generation was about more blades. The single blade was replaced with dual blades, which was replaced by three blades. Then four and now … yes, five blades! At some point, this approach is going to reach the point of diminishing returns—after all, you can only shave so close before it comes to cosmetic surgery.

So, where do you go from there? For Gillette, the marketing strategy will change from closeness of the shave to one of safety, comfort, and confidence. Gillette will keep the branding consistent—"the best a man can get"; but the changing strategy will move toward safety, convenience, and a subscription service (convenience) that will provide replacement cartridges.

Property and Casualty Insurance

Even the insurance industry is constantly evolving. Every several years, over the past 20 years, there has a been shift from one competing position to another in the interest of gaining market share. As a quick overview, the first objective for the insurance companies was to make sure they made money and could make necessary payments. That involved the traditional work of risk analysis, balance sheet management, etc.

Then the insurance industry shifted to a focus on delivering service and a variety of products. That involved expanding availability of agents and speedy claims processing. Then the industry shifted to a focus on bundling programs. Then the industry moved to value pricing and worked to meet these cost constraints by consolidating and adding technology and automation to the back room. As we're all aware, from the ubiquitous little GEICO Gecko and Flo with Progressive Insurance, insurance companies have been focused on their brands, direct selling to consumers, and marketing to small niches.

Ten Strategic Lessons

D'Aveni argues that globalization and technology have negated the long-held business strategies of finding a sustainable competitive advantage and competing by positioning your company's strength against a competitor's weakness. He explains that today's world requires stringing together a series of temporary competitive advantages. He's studied this for decades, examined dozens of industries, and given strategic advice to numerous companies and governments.

Here are the 10 strategic lessons D'Aveni has learned over the past three decades.

1. Globalization and technology (and to a lesser extent policy) have created a hypercompetitve world.

2. The speed of change continues to increase dramatically.

3. Business success will not be achieved with the old business strategies requiring long-term competitive advantages, nor by solely positioning strengths against a competitor's weaknesses.

4. Products will battle frequently for market share. Competitors will win by executing on a temporary advantage, and then executing on another temporary advantage, and so on.

5. Business victories will be achieved by a series of temporary advantages strung together in a sequence.

6. In a world competing on temporary advantages, the fierceness of competition goes way up.

7. The watchword of the future is disruption. The disruptive players will win the competition.

8. The availability of technology as a dynamic now favors offensive strategy versus defensive.

9. Strategy is about timing and speed of maneuvering.

10. The only way to a decisive victory—to trounce the competition—is to overwhelm the competitor's strength.*

* Here's something the old business rules don't mention: the truly decisive victory comes when "strength overwhelms strength," not when strength is used against a competitor's weakness. Using the tennis match as an example, D'Aveni explains "The goal is to run the other player ragged, tucker him out, and then hit the ball straight at him, so he realizes he can never win against you, and encourage him to go home with the goal of learning to play baseball."

Questions for Your Organization

Given the changing strategies necessary to compete in today's world, here are some questions for your organization.

- How have the wants of your market changed? How do you anticipate them changing over the next 5 to 10 years?

- What technologies, services, or other offerings from other industries could add value to your products?

- What can you do to better understand your customers' wants? When is the last time you asked your top 20 customers, "Tell us what you want" (taking copious notes)?

- What are the primary benefits of your offering? What are the marginal benefits your offering provides? (according to the customers).

- Is your company working on new offerings that really matter? Have you stopped work on offerings that don't?

- What does your product development process look like? What can be done to reduce the timeline?

- How could you change the basis of competition?

- What are the sequence of product disruptions you're going to introduce?

- How can you best bring those disruptions to market?

- What are the market positioning shifts you're going to introduce?

When considering the above, remember, the world is transforming before your eyes. The rapid change is taking place because hypercompetition is driven thru globalization and technology. It's not a bad world, but it is a disruptive world, where ongoing innovation and fierce competition are the new norm. If you don't drive change and compete fiercely, a competitor of yours will.

The good news is that you have the opportunity to make things better, to improve your organization and its products and services, to continuously innovate, to compete, and to lead the way.

No Bad Deals: Essential Negotiation Skills to Increase Effectiveness

I had the opportunity to meet Linda Ginzel, a clinical professor of managerial psychology at the University of Chicago Booth School of Business. Linda specialized in leadership development, organization behavior, and negotiation skills and was in New York City to lead a session on negotiation for One Day University.

At a fundamental level, it's been said that we are negotiating, any time two or more people divide resources or solve a problem—and most negotiations contain aspects of both competition and cooperation. Professor Ginzel explained that while people tend to default into a competitive position during the negotiation, the most economically desirable situation is to first "enlarge the pie" by creating joint gains. That is accomplished by cooperation.

Professor Ginzel's talk on negotiation was an eye-opener, anchored around an actual negotiation exercise that involved the approximately 300 attendees pairing off into groups of two. Each pairing consisted of an "A" and a "B" participant, each of whom had their own point schedule for negotiating a hypothetical annual corporate meeting that involved five issues for agreement: destination, accommodations, number of scheduled speakers, length of stay, and season. Each issue had five options (for example, there were five different destination options: Los Angeles, New Orleans, Atlanta,

Santa Fe, Orlando), and each option was worth different points for each of the two participants (Los Angeles might be worth 4,000 points for person "A" and 0 points for person "B"), and while you knew the point assignments for your options, the information was not shared with the other party.

The intended objective was to reach an agreement with your negotiation partner on the five issues (while keeping the point schedule confidential). If each person could not come up with at least 2,000 points, it was assumed that an outside party would be hired (if this were a real-world exercise) to do the negotiation. Within about 15 minutes, each side reached agreement on the five issues and were then able to compare their negotiated points. Typically, each person negotiated generally between 3,000 and 6,000 points.

Here's the interesting part, Professor Ginzel asked each two-person pairing to add their points together, which was a way of quantifying the total value of the negotiated deal. As in the example above, pairings typically totaled approximately 9,000 points, though some teams were considerably lower and others higher. In fact, there were some pairings whose totals were about 13,000 points—meaning they created considerably more overall value. Those pairings cooperatively enlarged the overall pie through dialogue, by avoiding sequentially moving down the list of five issues ("Let's settle the city first."), and by exploring ways to create value.

The 300 attendees were mostly seasoned executives; nonetheless, the large room was buzzing with the newly learned insights to creating value. Everybody knew the exercise was to reach agreement on the five issues. Yet judging by the clamor and discussion following the results, it's safe to say the vast majority of people never even thought about maximizing the total valuation while they were negotiating.

Here then are the six essential negotiation skills to increase effectiveness.

1. Prepare, prepare, prepare.
    Solid preparation is key. Gather as much information as you can about yourself and your counterparty. Identify issues, prioritize interests, and discuss best- and worst-case scenarios. Identify a list of questions to research.

2. Focus on interests, not positions.
    Build trust, share, and assess priorities. Ask lots of questions about interests, and listen carefully. Provide information, avoid unilateral concessions, and ask for reciprocity. Once we are willing and able to share information strategically with the goal of understanding underlying interests, we can make mutually beneficial trade-offs

rather than splitting the difference. Use compromise as a last resort, not as a goal.

3. Look for trade-offs to create value.
   Recognize that with many issues, joint gains are possible. Identify them. Differences are good in negotiations. Avoid sequential bargaining and single-issue offers. Keep all issues on the table for flexibility (perhaps use packaging options to help determine what's important to the other party). When we find the relative differences, we can trade on these differences. To find integrative outcomes, think like a trader—not a traitor!

4. Enlarge the pie before dividing.
   While we have a bias toward competition, most negotiations in life are mixed motive: they involve both competition (value claiming) and cooperation (value creating). Think creatively about putting new issues on the table; add side issues that benefit both parties. First, be cooperative to create value, and then competitive to claim value. You don't want to end up with a big slice of a small pie.

5. Adapt your strategy to your counterparty's style.
   Be aware that different problem-solving modes are available to you: competition, collaboration, accommodation, cooperation, compromise, and avoidance. Rather than relying on your default conflict resolution approach, practice being flexible and expand your repertoire. Remember to switch strategies when lacking progress.

6. Practice conditional cooperation.
   Be nice, but be clear that you will reciprocate competition with competition. Be forgiving (reciprocate cooperation). Don't be envious (don't compare your success relative to other players). Be clear (don't be too clever). Remember that tactics for creating value, such as revealing information and clearly communicating interests, might leave you open to competitive behavior from the other party.

Wanting to learn more, I asked Professor Ginzel how often the opportunity exists in the real-world to increase the overall value of a deal. She explained that unless it is a one-shot, single-item negotiation, there typically is the opportunity to enlarge the pie for both parties. An example might be negotiating a new job, where the position description might describe a director of engineering, but the company might be fully amenable to the more senior title of vice president of engineering—and that would cost them no additional compensation and might actually elevate the perceived level of the position—thereby being an example of "creating value."

Professor Ginzel explained that by adding issues that are valued differently by both parties, you increase the opportunity to make mutually beneficial trade (remember to "think like a trader"). In addition to things like job title, Professor Ginzel suggested other issues for consideration, such as vacation time, moving expenses, tuition reimbursement, six-month review, working from home, etc.

Given the scenario above, I asked Professor Ginzel if it was advisable to provide a general explanation to the other party at the start of the negotiation as to how you're looking to increase the overall pie. My concern was that without an explanation of why it might be in everybody's best interest to keep all issues on the table for flexibility, and explaining the concept of "increasing the pie"—the employer making the job offer might get the impression that the candidate is unable to commit to even the most basic elements of the offer—and thereby will be perceived as "flaky" or "difficult."

Her answer made great sense to me, as she said that she wouldn't feel the need to explain the strategy directly, and that doing so might in itself be perceived as "flaky" or "difficult." Recalling the quote from Ralph Waldo Emerson, "Your actions speak so loudly, I can not hear what you are saying," Professor Ginzel said she would allow her behavior during the negotiation (asking questions, understanding interests, thinking creatively, using reciprocity, etc.) to communicate her intention of being cooperative and flexible.

Professor Ginzel sees herself first and foremost as a teacher, and the session and subsequent conversations with her were educational and a real eye-opener. Yet, I wondered how this "value creation" business squares in the real rough and tumble world of business. We've heard the folklore of businesspeople being seemingly praised for their lopsided negotiation practices, where it wasn't enough to close the deal, but that the winning party actually wanted the other party to lose.

Professor Ginzel explained, "Creating value is more of a common practice than popular stories about tough negotiators would have you believe.

Remember that the definition of a successful negotiation in real life is repeat business and a good reputation (which helps you get that repeat business). If someone feels he/she has lost a negotiation, both parties have lost because of the reputation effect."

The Only Four Ways
You Can Ever Fail

I often think of the powerful words that Milton shouted into the wind on May 25, and I want those words to reverberate in my own head. Milton was 82 years old at the time, but I'm certain he yelled the words in a strong unwavering voice. A voice that carried the emotional mixture of joy, pride, wonder, and awe. And probably some fear and a bit of disbelief.

He shouted to be heard above the noise from the wind and the loud 12 horsepower, internal combustion engine straining right next to him. But mainly he shouted because of the pure exhilaration coursing through his being.

Milton Wright was the father of Orville and Wilbur, the famed American inventors and aviation pioneers who built, tested, and flew the first controlled "heavier-than-air flying machine" in 1903. It was just several years later, in 1910, that Milton shouted out the stirring words during the one and only time he ever flew.

If you get the chance, you should visit North Carolina and walk the grounds at Kill Devil Hills near Kitty Hawk. It's where the brothers spent month after month, year after year—assembling, testing, crashing, repairing, making slow incremental progress before doing more assembling, testing, crashing, repairing. It was there where the brothers first flew, and where we grew wings. We added the third dimension to our world. It's hallowed ground.

Early flight was dangerous, pioneering work and Milton had made his sons promise to never fly together. He couldn't imagine losing them both during a flight crash. Over the subsequent decades, aeronautical engineers and historians have thoroughly studied and chronicled what the Wright brothers did to succeed. Searching "Wright brothers" on Amazon yields 1,628 books.

But, when considering what contributed to the success of these bicycle mechanics and self-taught engineers, both of whom didn't even graduate from high school, it's also important to consider what they decided not to do.

Here are the four things they didn't do.

1. Obsess over milestones.

   Their intent was to fly. But they had no real idea how long it'd take to work their way through the innumerable challenges. For one thing, they calculated they'd need a minimum of eight horsepower from an engine that weighed less than 200 pounds. There was no such engine available at the time. So the brothers set about building one.

   Not to mention the other innumerable obstacles involved with creating a lightweight wood and cloth structure that would withstand the forces encountered while flying; or how to alter the shape of the wing surfaces so their flight could be controlled.

   The only thing greater than the unanswered questions and problems was their commitment to get it all figured out. What they didn't have was an unrealistic schedule.

2. Work haphazardly.

   Anders Ericsson is an internationally recognized professor of psychology at Florida State University, who has spent a lifetime researching and studying human achievement and performance. He's studied world-class experts in a variety of areas, including athletics, music, chess, medicine, etc.

   What Professor Ericsson has found is that the best way to improve and become a master in your life's work is through purposeful (or dedicated) practice. He has authored several books, most recently *Peak: Secrets from the New Science of Expertise*, published in 2016. Simply stated Ericsson describes purposeful practice as having four important primary components: a specific goal, intense focus, immediate feedback, and frequent incremental improvements.

   The Wright brothers are nearly a perfect example for all of these components.

3. Chase someone else's goal.

   Their objective of flying wasn't assigned to them. It wasn't the goal of some wealthy industrialist who pressured the brothers to solve the challenge of flight. It wasn't a directive from an existing business enterprise looking for a new way to transport paying customers.

Learning to fly was their goal. The seeds originated in 1878 when their father brought home a small toy helicopter for Orville and Wilbur, then just seven and nine years old. The boys played constantly with the rubber band-powered toy until it broke, at which point they built their own.

4. Quit.

Enough said.

Although Milton made his sons promise they'd never fly together, there was just one exception ever made to that rule. Orville and Wilbur flew together on May 25, 1910. The brothers landed safely. Afterwards, Orville took up their father, Milton, for his one and only flight. The 82-year-old Milton climbed aboard the flyer and held on tightly as it accelerated across the ground.

As Orville powered the aircraft upward, Milton looked down and watched everything he'd ever known in all his 82 years, slowly fall away. He saw the clumps of grass and the leaves on the trees merge into blocks of solid colors. He saw plots of land. He saw how the fencing created lines across the terrain below. He watched a small flock of startled birds take off from a field and fly under the Wright plane. Everything Milton had ever known was below him, as though it were spread out on a giant, flat canvas.

I wonder if his first and only experience flying generated a glimpse of a new world of possibilities. If at some point during the flight, Milton sensed a transition. Certainly the Wrights knew their invention would result in enormous changes in the world below.

During the flight, Milton turned his head, and looked at his son, Orville. So that Milton could be heard above the wind and the engine noise—and the din of the beliefs and limitations that held our bare feet to the warm, hard earth over the millennia—Milton shouted to his son.

"Higher, Orville, higher!"

PART FOUR

Courage and Creativity

Taking Stock and Standing Up; Discovering and Connecting

What It Feels Like to Punch Fear in the Face

Seems like most everybody makes excuses. Or is afraid to wrestle with themselves until the old self lies exhausted in the dirt, yelling "uncle" … and the new self stands up, walks away, and doesn't look back. Here's one person who doesn't make excuses and continues to punch fear in the face.

Chuck Close is a world-renowned artist. He paints large-scale portraits, measuring several feet on each side. And his portrait paintings are so impossibly and unimaginably detailed, that they're mistaken for photographs.[44]

But, even if Chuck Close knew you as a dear and close friend, he probably wouldn't recognize you. Close has what neurologists call prosopagnosia. It's believed to be caused by lesions that have damaged the brain. It's also called face blindness. Here's what that means. Chuck Close isn't able to recognize faces. It's why, even after years of being married to his wife, Close didn't recognize her.

You'd think this rare condition would make it more difficult to paint portraits. But according to Close, that thought didn't even occur to him. Close said,

"I was not conscious of making a decision to paint portraits because I have difficulty recognizing faces. That occurred to me twenty years after the fact when I looked at why I was still painting portraits, why that still had urgency for me. I began to realize that it has sustained me for so long because I have difficulty in recognizing faces."[45]

And if that weren't enough, there were other major difficulties that would impact his ability to create art. In 1988, after delivering a speech in New York City, Chuck Close had what he has come to describe as "the incident." A spinal artery collapse resulted in him having a seizure. It was cataclysmic, and Close lost essentially all movement from the neck down.

Close worked hard for months in physical therapy, but only regained a minimal amount of movement in his arms. He would have to spend the rest of his life in a motorized wheelchair. But his desire to create burned within him, and, fortunately, Chuck Close was driven to try. So he strapped a paintbrush to his wrist and went to work using what little movement he had. As is the case with all real artists, his work evolved.

Close continued painting portraits on large canvasses. But now he had an assistant begin by dividing the canvas into small grids. And with a brush strapped to his wrist, Close utilized paint and paper in each grid to create a small work of art. And each grid contributed a piece to the overall portrait. The resulting image was pixelated—and compelling.

Here's what Chuck Close can teach you about what it feels like to stare down fear.

It Takes Courage

Imagine this. You have honed your skills to the point where you can paint a face on a nine-foot by seven-foot canvas with such exacting detail, that it is mistaken for a photograph. Then you lose all those skills. And yet somehow, you have the wherewithal to make the decision to start all over again, fully knowing that whatever you do, will have to be done with a small fraction of the capability you once had.

The magnitude of courage necessary to move forward is frankly hard to fathom. To better understand how daunting this must have been, imagine other professions that require decades of neuromuscular training before attaining world-class performance—ballerina, football player, or race car driver—and after experiencing what Chuck Close did, they decide to begin again.

Success Is Uncertain

Of course it is. That's why you're afraid.

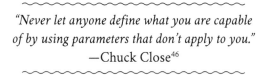

"Never let anyone define what you are capable
of by using parameters that don't apply to you."
—Chuck Close[46]

It's Hard

Ditto. Maybe unimaginably hard. Begin the work.

Nobody Can Do It for You

Nobody could pick up a brush and paint while Chuck Close sat nearby giving instructions. That's coaching or teaching, not painting. What's more, nobody but Close could experience the struggle that would shape his work into something entirely new.

It Leads to New Possibilities

What a loss it would have been if Chuck Close stopped making art after his incident. Instead, he strapped a brush to his hand and continued. In the process, he created a new way of seeing and thinking about portraits—and created hundreds of new paintings.

There Is a Choice

Looking over some of the paintings Chuck Close has done since his incident, it's kind of impossible to imagine that he might have made the decision to *not* paint. But, of course, he could have made the understandable decision to never paint again.

It's good he made the choice to continue. And not just because the world is inspired by his work. But because it would certainly have been a dire world for Chuck Close if he did not make the decision to continue to create.

"I don't work with inspiration. Inspiration
is for amateurs. I just get to work."
—Chuck Close[47]

It's Never Over (As Long as You're Alive and Creating)

Although Chuck Close is nearly 80 years old (he was born in 1940), he's still on the journey of reinvention. In the past couple of years, he has separated from his wife, relocated to a geographic area far from the comfort and support of his many friends, and he continues to experiment with his art to the point that he's dismaying art critics and confounding friends.

And here's what Chuck Close knows. Life isn't about finding yourself. Life is about creating yourself.[48]

Five Daily Practices to Unleash Your Creativity Mojo

I wasn't smart enough. Probably not even cool enough. But I wanted in.

The streetlights cast an eerie glow along the dark street. I hid in the shadows and watched closely as a man walked up to the steel door and knocked. At about head height, a small panel on the door slid open. I could see a woman peering out. She said "twelve." The man responded "six." The door opened.

I waited in the silence for several minutes, until it happened again. This time a woman approached the door. After knocking, the panel slid open, and the woman inside said "six." The reply was "three." The door opened.

I had it figured out! I walked confidently up to the door and knocked. The panel opened, the woman said "eight," to which I replied "four." And … and … nothing. The door remained locked.

Maybe if I'd have spent more time strengthening my creativity, and doing these daily practices, I would've been able to solve the puzzle and open the door.

1. Do something different.

   We're all creatures of habit. That's generally a good thing, as it allows us to efficiently zip through the day and avoid the continual awkwardness of being outside our comfort zone. But those habits also curtail new experiences, and new experiences are what keep us learning and yield new discoveries.

   Famous record producer Sam Phillips combined different styles of music in new ways. And that continual search led to the discovery of new talent and new music. Sam Phillips discovered talent and shaped seminal artists that included Howlin' Wolf, Carl Perkins, Jerry Lee

Lewis, and an 18-year-old truck driver named Elvis Presley. He helped create rock 'n' roll along the way.

Making a point of doing just one new thing a day can have a big effect. Try it for a week and maybe keep it going for a lifetime. Brush your teeth using the opposite hand. Sit with a different group at lunch. Make some rock 'n' roll, and remember what Sam Phillips said, "If you're not doing something different, you're not doing anything."

2. Take a break.
Step away from the problem and stop racking your brain for a solution. There's a reason so many good ideas come to us in the morning or in the shower. We're rested and we've given our brains time to process. Take a walk, or get outside for a run. Listen to music, or pick up an instrument and make some music.

Or try meditation. Tough guy actor Hugh Jackman, who played the Marvel comics superhero Wolverine, says "Meditation is all about the pursuit of nothingness. It's like the ultimate rest. It's better than the best sleep you've ever had. It's a quieting of the mind. It sharpens everything, especially your appreciation of your surroundings. It keeps life fresh."

I like the idea of quieting the mind and sharpening everything. Besides, who am I to argue with Wolverine.

3. Learn something new (in your chosen area of expertise).
When I first started out as an engineer, I was told by a grumpy old draftsman as he stood over his drawing board, that "I've forgotten more than you know." I was fresh out of engineering school, so that was true. But the comment still kinda stung.

The point is, those days of knowing-it-all are gone. Things are changing so fast in today's world, that you have to continually be learning. You have to keep yourself on the learning curve. Don't wait until you're forced to learn a new skill. Don't whine about it. Make learning a part of who you are.

If you learn something new in your chosen field every day ... that's 364 new things in a year (you get your birthday off). Yes, I did the math. Fairly soon, all those bits of knowledge will start to connect with one another, reinforcing and deepening your understanding on the topic. Before you know it, you'll be a subject matter expert!

And maybe, at some point in the distant future, your brain will overflow with knowledge, and you'll have forgotten more than someone else even knows. But don't forget the important stuff. Like remembering to call your mom, being kind, and offering encouragement.

4. **Venture outside your comfort zone.**
    Whether it's entrepreneur Richard Branson, boxer Manny Pacquiao, physicist Stephen Hawking or the band U2—everyone I deeply admire has had to grind through to success. They basically had to influence and shape the reality around them, at the same time improve themselves such that they could accomplish what they set out to do. Experience shows that deliberate practice is what makes great accomplishment possible.
    These might be bumper-sticker slogans, but worth remembering.

    - If you still look cute after your workout, you're not training hard enough.

    - If you don't make mistakes, you're not working on hard enough problems.

    And that means spending the majority of your development time outside your comfort zone.

    How about this for a bumper sticker? "Be the most determined person you know."

5. **Try a new approach.**
    Pablo Picasso achieved the pinnacle of his success when he invented Cubism. He achieved fame and fortune and was revered not just within the art community but in the world. And then at the peak of his fame, Picasso decided he's no longer interested in that style he created. He went back to Italy and studied the artists from the past. It was described as the equivalent of going back to kindergarten.
    This might actually be the most difficult of all. Force yourself to approach a problem from an entirely new perspective. Few people continually reinvent over the course of their careers. Walt Disney said, "We keep moving forward, opening new doors, and doing new things, because we're curious and curiosity keeps leading us down new paths."

    So, be careful when you catch yourself saying "Yea, I like [insert accomplished person here], but I like her older stuff better." You just might be saying that you're more comfortable with the familiar, and [insert accomplished person here] is continuing to grow and leaving you behind.

Which brings me back to the door …

The first time the panel slid open, "twelve" was answered with "six."

The second time, "six" was answered with "three."

It turns out, the answer for "eight" … is "five."

You see, I thought the answer was to divide by two, but actually the answer was simpler.

The answer was simply the number of letters in the word.

A Proven Technique for Producing Ideas

The most recorded song in history arrived in a dream. The melody was truly beautiful. A wholly formed composition of chords that immediately produced profound sentimental longing in the listener. It was so complete, that it sounded familiar even with the first listen.

It was 1963, and Paul McCartney was 21.

"I fell out of bed. I had a piano by my bedside and I must have dreamed it because I tumbled out of bed and put my hands on the piano keys and I had a tune in my head. It was just all there, a complete thing. I couldn't believe it, it came too easy."[49]

The song seemed so familiar to Paul, that he wondered if he'd heard it elsewhere. So he played the melody for the other Beatles. They told him they'd never heard it anywhere else. He played it for other musicians and friends.

"In fact I didn't believe I'd written it. I thought maybe I'd heard it before, it was some other tune, and I went round for weeks playing the chords of the song for people, asking them, 'Is this like something? I think I've written it.' And people would say, 'No, it's not like anything else, but it's good.'"[50]

Paul said it felt like he was "handing in something you'd found at the police station and waiting to see if anyone claimed it. After two weeks they hadn't in this case so I felt entitled to collect it and call it my property."[51]

But the lyrics needed work. In fact, they were nonsensical. "Scrambled eggs, Oh you've got such lovely legs, Scrambled eggs. Oh, my baby, how I love your legs."[52]

So Paul worked on the lyrics, and in 1965 sat down with an acoustic Epiphone guitar and recorded the song. The song was reworked with the help of the legendary producer George Martin. George Martin described that song as a transformative event in the music of the Beatles.

The song "Yesterday" went on to be the most recorded song in history. It has been recorded by over 2,200 different artists, including Frank Sinatra, James Taylor, The Supremes, Elvis, Marvin Gaye, Ray Charles, Bob Dylan, and Linkin Park, to name but several.

Coincidentally, it was also in 1965 that a brief and simple book came out titled *A Technique for Producing Ideas*, by James Webb Young. At the time of its publication, Young was regarded as a creative wizard in the advertising industry, and his book described the simple process for generating ideas experienced by many creative people. In the course of this brief and inexpensive $5 book, Young explained and systemized the five stages to producing ideas.

James Young knew the five-stage technique worked and even considered not sharing what he'd learned so as to maintain an advantage over his competition in the advertising industry. But in the end, he believed that the positive good of sharing the technique far outweighed any downside related to the fear of aiding his competition.

Besides, he explained that the five-stage formula is so simple, that "few who hear it actually believe it." And that executing on the formula, despite the fact that the technique provides a path to success, does require intellectual work, such that "not all who accept it use it." It's a process that has been used by countless creative people.

It's exactly the technique McCartney instinctively used in creating the song "Yesterday." And it's undoubtedly a technique that you've used in your life and work—though you might not even have been aware of the actual process.

Here's a summary of the five-step technique that James Webb wrote in his book, *A Technique for Producing Ideas*.

1. Gathering

   This is the fact-finding stage. You gather information and educate yourself about the matter. In the book, James Young is careful to stress that this means going deep beyond what might typically be expected to fully immerse yourself in the challenge.

What are the real needs facing the customer? What is the heart of the question? What are the real barriers? How are similar matters being addressed elsewhere in related areas?

Fact finding might involve technology, customer insights, service issues, or even entire business models. This initial stage is where the more information obtained, even from seemingly afield, the better.

Although everyone acknowledges the importance of truly understanding the problem and gathering specific knowledge about possible solutions, this involves tedious work. In the haste for an answer or solution, the fact-gathering stage is easily shortchanged.

Relevant to McCartney, this stage is exemplified by the countless thousands of hours spent listening, playing, and writing music throughout his life.

2. Thinking
Once all the facts have been gathered, this is the stage where thinking and problem solving are applied. This is the stage where the different aspects of the challenge are considered.

This is the time to delve deep into what might work and also to think broadly about different potential solutions. The greater the number and variety of possible approaches and different combinations considered, the better.

3. Incubation
At this stage of the process, you actually stop the deliberate and conscious thinking about the matter, and essentially hand the work over to your creative unconscious mind. James Young recommends purposely doing other things—like going to the movies or art museums—to give your brain the freedom to think creatively.

This is what happened to Paul McCartney when he was sleeping.

4. The Solution!
During a morning shower, or a run in the woods, or in our sleep—the idea emerges. Sometimes in a flash, sometimes with a hesitant. almost shy appearance. The facts and concepts have been associating and connecting in our brain, and the idea emerges from our subconscious.

James Young calls this the "eureka!" moment.

It's what physicist Niels Bohr experienced when he went to sleep and dreamed about atoms. He saw a nucleus and electrons spinning around the center, like planets around a star. After waking, he believed the vision was an accurate depiction, so he went about finding the evidence to support this theory.

5. Final Development
This is where the additional work is applied to bring the idea to fruition in the real world. It's when McCartney swapped out the lyrics of "Scrambled eggs, Oh you've got such lovely legs" for "Yesterday, all my troubles seemed so far away." It's when George Martin pushed for a string accompaniment to the song.

In a world where our problems require new thinking, your best creative self is essential, and the simple techniques outlined in the $5 (or less) book could be of great benefit to you (and the world). Spend 30 minutes (it's only 40 short pages) and give it a read. The writing might seem a bit dated, but the words of wisdom are timeless.

You'll increase your chances of having sweet dreams. And the results could be significant. Maybe that's what Paul McCartney meant when he wrote "And when the night is cloudy there is still a light that shines on me. Shine on 'til tomorrow, let it be."

And, by the way, the song "Let It Be" was inspired by another of Paul McCartney's dreams. He was dreaming of his mother, who died from cancer when he was just 14. He said, "It was great to visit with her again. I felt blessed to have that dream."

Becoming a Creative Genius (Again)

Scientists know quite a bit about the human brain. And more important, they know about your brain (yes, your specific brain). It weighs just over three pounds, makes up just 2 percent of your weight, and contains about 86 billion nerve cells (neurons) that are connected by trillions of connections, or synapses. It's the most complex structure in the universe.

It's our brains that let us humans shape essentially every facet of our world. Our brains allow us to communicate complex ideas, recognize a single face from a billion others, build rockets that fly into outer space, and make us feel all fluttery when we get near someone we love.

Recent advances using functional magnetic resonance imaging (fMRI) are giving scientists new insights into how the brain works by allowing real-time visualization of activity in the different regions of the brain. But the reality is, it's all still early pioneering work. The brain—including how consciousness and memories and intelligence work—remains a great mystery.

But one thing scientists do know fairly well is how to test for creative ingenuity. How to find those seemingly rare individuals who are "the creative types"—the problem solvers, musicians, artists, philosophers, designers, and poets. In fact, scientists can determine quite accurately which people belong to that rarified most creative category.

And here's the unbelievable truth—you belong in that genius category. Those are your cohorts. Your people.

In the 1960s, NASA had a mission to land a man on the Moon, and the NASA deputy director hired a scientist named George Land to devise a creativity test to determine the most innovative and creative NASA engineers. The test Land developed proved to be of exceptional accuracy, and NASA used the assessment to determine its most creative engineers and program managers, before assigning them to various projects.

In 1968, Land decided, really out of curiosity, to try the same creativity test on a group of five-year-old children. The results were both unexpected and astounding. To Land's astonishment, he found that 98 percent of the kids tested at the creative genius level.

Five years later, Dr. Land tested the same group of kids at 10 years old. This time, the percentage scoring a genius rating dropped to 30 percent. Land tested the group again when they were 15 years old. This time the percentage scoring as geniuses dropped to 12 percent.

And what percentage of adults scored as creative geniuses? Over the years, the test has been applied to over 280,000 adults, and 2 percent of the adults tested as creative geniuses.

George Land described these continual and significant decreases in scoring as a result of creativity being essentially manufactured out by our educational system. In other words, the process of educating kids in school results in "de-genius-ing" them. Land believed that part of this is because we teach children to simultaneously think divergent and convergent.

Divergent thinking is when you're brainstorming and exploring a multitude of possible ideas. Where idea generation means casting a wide net. Where nothing is off limits.

Convergent thinking is when you're pruning away the different ideas, attempting to narrow the thinking to a final working solution.

Land explains that simultaneously thinking divergently and convergently results in immediate restriction and even dismissal of the various ideas as they emerge. As soon as someone has the inkling of a possible idea, he or she is immediately evaluating and eliminating the idea as too complicated, costly, unfeasible, or "far-out."

Clearly, we adults need help. My friend, Carl Nordgren, has taught creativity and entrepreneurship at Duke University for 14 years. He is also a successful entrepreneur, novelist, and an experienced fishing guide. He knows how to lure a prize creative idea and a rainbow trout that's hidden beneath the surface. Nordgren wrote an informative and important book called *Becoming a Creative Genius {Again}*, and he can help us regain our creativity.

Here are just five of the many ways Nordgren advises we get reacquainted with our creative genius younger selves.

1. Start a creative action program (CAP).

    Simply, this means doing something new every day and making a note of it. It doesn't need to be complicated or time-consuming. In fact, it likely won't take any extra time. One day it could be driving a different way to work. Another day, using your other hand to brush your teeth. Or cooking a new Indian dinner. Setting the alarm 45 minutes earlier and going for a run. Giving meditation a try. Delaying checking email until you've planned your day. Jotting down a list of ideas to make your workday more productive. Even small efforts like those will begin stimulating your creativity. By making a point of doing one new thing every day, you'll develop a mindset of looking for new things to try.

2. Keep a journal. Make observations.

    Get a notebook and carry it around with you. Have the intention of being observant, jotting down ideas that might occur during the day. Keep it casual. Don't worry about filling it with brilliant thoughts. Note whatever creative observations you might have on a particular day. Or jot down a recurring question you want to get answered. Or your thoughts about how something at work could be improved. Write, sketch, scribble, and doodle. Aim for at least a few entries each week.

3. Practice, ready, fire, aim.

    As adults, we often overthink things. Doing the standard, "ready, aim, aaaaim." Once I participated in a workshop where at one point we broke into groups of several people. We were to construct a tower, of maximum height, using just Play-Doh and straws. We had 10 minutes. The only rule was that the first six minutes were for planning and discussion only. We weren't allowed to touch the Play-Doh or the straws until the final two minutes allotted for "build" time.

    For the first six minutes, we planned the hell out of that structure and discussed dividing the construction tasks. When it came time to build, there was a frenzy of elbows. When the clock ran out on our four-minute build time—our planned masterpiece was totally incomplete and lay in pieces on the desk.

    Another group (who was in another room and had not observed

our experience) was given the same 10 minutes, but was told to begin building immediately. They crushed us with a wobbly structure that stood several feet tall.

It's not a perfectly applicable example for everything. But it did make the point of getting caught-up in "aiming" and the advantage of getting started "firing."

4. Be generous.

   Give and contribute without regard for credit. Listen intently when other people share their ideas and suggestions. Support them. Build on their ideas.

   Carl Nordgren urges his students to do this.

   "Become known for giving what must be the greatest gift of all these days, their undivided attention, and practice being generous listeners. That means focused listening, blocking out all distractions, and putting your phone away.

   And it also means carefully listening, for the best the idea has to offer."[53]

5. Be playful.

   The one thing that is self-evident of creative geniuses (and I'm talking about those five year olds) is that they know how to play. How to be curious. How to explore. Follow their lead, and become a creative genius (again). The kids are waiting, and they want you to reach 98 percent.

How to Kill a Good Idea

One time, I blindly stepped into an elevator shaft on the twelfth floor. I was working in Houston, Texas, and the company had recently moved into a new building where several floors were still being completed. To deal with all the construction material, the elevator interiors were lined with thick blankets, giving them the gray appearance of the shaft itself. What's more, the elevators didn't always work properly. We were told an electrician was killed working on one of the elevators a couple of weeks previously.

I was carrying a two foot tall stack of computer printouts that nearly came up to my chin. The stack blocked my downward view, and when the elevator doors opened with an audible ding, I didn't even think of looking down, but rather just stepped in. With nothing under my feet, I began to fall. That was a surprise. But more about that in a minute …

I've seen my share of good ideas die. Occasionally, how they die comes as a complete surprise. Like my misstep into the elevator shaft, or the twist ending of a whodunit mystery that you never saw coming. Like when you learn in *The Empire Strikes Back* that Darth Vader is Luke Skywalker's dad.

But, product innovation isn't scripted like a movie. It happens in the real world and is subject to all the inane and myopic thinking that people are known to often exhibit. I've been guilty of it too. Like the time in the mid-1990s, when I wondered to myself (thankfully) why a junior colleague was so enthusiastic about the company getting a Web page.

In contrast to the surprise movie ending, the vast majority of the time these innovation casualties don't happen in a single climactic scene with everyone caught off guard. Rather, their demise comes as no surprise to anyone. Not only that, but everyone usually knows what killed it.

In *The Hound of the Baskervilles*, Sir Arthur Conan Doyle wrote, "The world is full of obvious things which nobody by any chance ever observes." Anyone who's fought to bring innovative products to fruition can deduce that Sherlock Holmes never had a case involving product development; otherwise he might have said, "New product development is resisted by many and usually in full view of everyone."

It usually doesn't take a detective to figure out the cause of death. Here's a list of the usual suspects.

1. Apathy

   The truth is that companies are filled with people who mostly don't care one way or the other about the next product introduction. Of course, they'll never admit that to their colleagues. On the contrary, they probably outwardly appear to be quite enthusiastic about the innovation and will do the work that's asked of them to advance the cause. Just like they do with anything they're working on.

   But here's the thing. Bringing a new technology to fruition is *not* just like anything else being worked on. In fact, it's quite *unlike* anything else. It's a new product. It hasn't been figured out. And new things only become successful when there's an inordinate amount of work applied to moving the project along, to overcoming new problems (everything is hard the first time), and pushing through the many iterations it's going to take to succeed. By definition, it's not like anything you're already doing.

2. Jealousy

   It's human nature, but sometimes people don't want something (or someone) to succeed. It could be because they're resentful of who came up with the idea. Maybe the idea originated in another department ("What does Sales know?") or from a customer ("Customers don't know the market") or from someone who's young, or old, or whatever.

3. Lack of Commitment and Effort

   Many people on the team care about what's being developed and the company's continued success. They genuinely cheer for the day the new product will be released. They love the idea of a new product, but their enthusiasm wanes when demands start affecting their normal workday. They resist putting in the time to meet the needs, not to mention giving their blood, sweat, and tears.

   Pushing an innovation along the path to success means occasional (or frequent) early or late days or working weekends. It means intense periods of focus. Thinking differently than you do when managing your existing work. Often it means going the extra mile, and sometimes it means taking the shortcut through the woods.

4. Limited Resources
    I used to tell the team (proudly), "We've done so much, with so little, for so long, that we can now do anything with nothing." We've all been asked to do more with less. Less people, less budget, less external resources, less time, less physical space, less whatever. And yes, you can rally and get a lot done despite the shortcomings. But, as we all know, creating a breakthrough is hard work. And while you might have to work with limited resources, it's unrealistic for the company to expect you to pull a rabbit out of a hat, if you're not even given a hat. At some point, limited resources are not only just challenging, but they cross the line into planning to fail.

5. Politics
    People oppose things all the time for the wrong reasons—to protect their turf or simply to express their authority against a threatening influence. Once I was chastised by a colleague who headed another department for calling someone in his group on her mobile phone at 5:20 p.m. during her drive home. The department head said I was violating her private information by asking for her mobile number. Territorial attitudes aren't helpful in getting things done.

6. Aversion to Change
    Industrialist J. Paul Getty was right when he said, "In times of rapid change, experience could be your worst enemy." It's often the most experienced people who are the most resistant to change. But the bottom line is this: people get comfortable doing things a certain way, and as a result are participants in putting up resistance to what's new.

7. Ignorance
    I've seen people fight something new, simply because they don't really understand it. Or they have no ability to distinguish between something critical versus unimportant. It's like the anecdote about a $1 part holding up a million-dollar Space Shuttle launch. I've seen people delay a new product because it didn't yet have its own

accounting charge code, and they didn't want to bill their time to a general charge code.

8. Lack of Courage (Fear)
    Nobody will ever admit that they're afraid of innovation (or change). But the fear of trying something new, and failing, is ubiquitous. It's often the reason for protracted product testing or failure to ship.

Any of the above suspects can be used to kill innovation, and usually more than one is at work simultaneously. Their danger is easily overlooked for a couple of reasons. For one thing, everything on the list is common and familiar. We experience resistance so much that we almost don't recognize the pull toward oblivion. It's like a gravitational constant in our work environment. Maybe like an open elevator door we step through every day. Another reason these dangers are overlooked is that they're observable by everyone. And that shared awareness makes them feel less threatening.

Despite the above list of suspects waiting to kill your idea, hard work and awareness will help you avoid them. And, of course, sometimes we get lucky. Which is what happened to me in the elevator. The elevator indeed had malfunctioned. But, fortunately, my fall into the abyss was short, as it had stopped a foot below the level of the floor. Decades later, I can tell you, nonetheless, it was a memorable drop. I collected my wits and the computer printouts that had fallen to the floor, promising myself that in the future—I'd look where I was going.

"Elementary, my dear Watson!"

The Twelve Dimensions of Courage

I'd only been out of college for a few years, when my manager made an offhand comment that has stayed with me for decades. He said, "I like to take words apart to better understand myself." His name was Alan. I don't remember his last name, but I remember he used to talk slowly—like he was thinking about every word. He seemed old, though looking back, he was probably in his late thirties. I asked him what he meant. "Well, I'll give you a real example," he said, "one from just the other day."

We worked at a large aerospace company outside Los Angeles. My desk was made of gray sheet metal and was in the middle of a cornfield-size room with hundreds of other identical gray desks arranged in a grid on the linoleum-tiled floor. It was a strange place, full of unusual characters. An old engineer, used to remove the cap from a BIC pen and nonchalantly scrape wax from his ear canals while talking to you. On one occasion, I earnestly asked someone named "JP Smith" what the initials stood for in his first name. He became enraged and yelled, "Those aren't initials. That is the name my parents gave me, and it doesn't stand for anything!" Another guy whistled made-up tunes—*continuously*. I mean, he always whistled. It was torture. To this day, hearing someone whistling makes me cringe.

In comparison to the other people surrounding me in the cavernous cubicle farm, Alan was normal. We were in his office. It was one of several cubes, which had seven-foot walls but no ceilings, that formed a row alongside the open floor plan. He took out a sandwich from a paper bag and while eyeing it said, "Take the word discourage." He exaggerated the prefix dis. "Well, the *dis* is Latin for apart. So, whenever I might be feeling *dis*-couraged," he continued, "I ask myself 'Do I want to be the kind of person that's apart or separated from courage?'"

I nodded in understanding. For whatever reason, I've thought about that conversation occasionally over the past 30 years. And during that time, whenever I read about someone with courage, or saw someone act heroically, I would think about Alan's comment and the difference between courage and *dis*courage.

Here's what I think courage often looks like. These are just rough guidelines, of course. A fundamental reality of having courage is that it's available to anyone. There are no age, sex, race, religion, or cultural requirements. And there's no *one* way (or even twelve) to be courageous. But this is a start.

1. Staring Down the Fear

   Sooner or later, we're all going to be face to face with something we'd rather not be facing. Loss of a job, illness, economic calamity, natural disaster, death of someone we love. You name it. It's not that courageous people don't feel fear, it's that at some point, they decide to stare it down and punch fear in the face.

2. Speaking Up

   Not everybody has an equal voice. Not everybody sees what you do. When Beatle George Harrison learned about the starvation and suffering in Bangladesh, he decided to use his voice for those without one. George helped organize the first charity concert, the Concert for Bangladesh in Madison Square Garden in 1971.

   In addition to raising visibility and money, the Concert for Bangladesh was the model for all future benefit concerts. In his book, *1,000 Recordings to Hear Before You Die*, author Tom Moon wrote, "Pull this out whenever your faith in the power of music begins to wane."[54]

   You don't have to look far to find someone without a voice. Speak up for them.

3. Silence

   *"Courage is what it takes to stand up and speak;
   courage is also what it takes to sit down and listen."*
   —Winston Churchill

4. Solitude

   It's difficult to stand apart from the crowd, to be the lone voice, to go where you're not supposed to go. It's easy to get behind the curtain (symbol or dogma or culture of the times) and repeat what everyone else is saying.

5. Supportive

   It's easy to be critical. To shout or mumble (or tweet) why something or someone has failed. To pile on the criticism, while secure in anonymity, authority, or distance. A courageous person recognizes bravery in others, and doesn't stand on the sidelines taking cheap shots.

"Any fool can criticize, condemn and complain—and most fools do."
—Benjamin Franklin

---

6. Saying No Thanks

   If you want to separate yourself from the pack of mediocrity, you can't spend all your time in the pack. You need the confidence and commitment to invest your time elsewhere. Saying "yes" to everything is going to make that difficult. It's hard to separate yourself from the pack, if you're always putting yourself in the pack. And it's nearly impossible to find the time, if you're always pursuing other people's suggestions.

   Consider Russian cellist Daniil Shafran who, after spending countless hours practicing, won first prize at the USSR All-Union Competition for Violinists and Cellists. It was all the more amazing as he was 14 years old and had entered unofficially because he was below the qualifying age limit.

   Shafran would often practice a song at twice the speed to challenge himself technically. He described his attitude as, "mercilessly strict with myself when practicing." Shafran, as required of any world-class performer, had the courage to put in the countless hours necessary to master his craft and passed up lots of other activities along the way.

7. Stepping Forward

   Courageous behavior requires people to take their turn.

   When someone fell onto the New York City subway tracks at the 72nd Street Broadway-Seventh Avenue station and was knocked unconscious, Gray Davis, a dancer with the American Ballet Theater said he, "initially waited for somebody else to jump down there. People were screaming to get help. But nobody jumped down. So I jumped down."

Once on the tracks, Mr. Davis lifted the unconscious man onto the platform, and then heard the coming train in the distance. "It was really scary," he said. "I don't know if I had time to process it until I saw my wife coming down crying—then I realized it was scary."[55]

The opposite, of course, is shirking from taking your turn. Hoping you won't be asked to do something uncomfortable because you don't want to look stupid, awkward, or ill-prepared (much less do something dangerous).

8. Searching
Courageous people are often seeking new ways to improve and new horizons to explore.

Alexandra David-Néel was a Belgian-French explorer and writer of over 30 books about Eastern religion, philosophy, and her travels. Her work influenced writers Jack Kerouac and Allen Ginsberg. To say she lived an adventurous life would be an understatement. She first ran away at age five, wrote an anarchist treatise that was translated into five languages, slept on a bed of nails, and lived in caves. In 1924, she snuck into the Forbidden City. Foreigners were barred from traveling to Lhasa, Tibet, so David-Néel disguised herself as a beggar and then a monk by smearing her face with soot and wearing a traditional fur hat—and then hid a pistol and a compass under her yak wool rags.

Other people exhibit their courage not by exploring inaccessible foreign lands, but by exploring their inner psychology, or musical soundscapes, or solutions to unsolved math problems.

9. Standing Your Ground
Courageous people reach a point where they say, "enough is enough," and decide that they're no longer going to continue forgoing what they believe should be theirs. This stance is often directed not toward an external enemy, but toward themselves. They demand of themselves, "Will the real me please step forward?"

This is what Eric Thomas, a homeless high school dropout, asked of himself—before he went on to get his high school equivalency, then a college degree, then a master's degree, and then a doctoral degree.

10. Saying You're Sorry

Being human entails making mistakes. And when you're living courageously, that necessitates trying and doing things above and beyond what's normal. So, yes, there is the inevitability of falling short or screwing up. Accept responsibility. Apologize. Learn. Move on. It's what brave people do.

11. Staying the Course

American writer and educator George Leonard outlined what the path to mastery looks like in his excellent book by the same title. His conclusion has been proven by neuroscientists and extreme performance coaches and athletes (and our own experiences). Progress is taking place even when there's not obvious external evidence of improvement. When time is spent, seemingly grinding along on the long stretch of the plateau.

12. Starting

I'll end at the beginning. At some point, being courageous means getting started. The first step is often the scariest and the most difficult. But without that first step, there is no courageous act.

I left that aerospace company a couple of years after working for Alan, and we never connected again. It's been more than a few decades. My hope is he's healthy and happy. Wherever he is, I know he's not *dis*-couraged.

Why You Should Speak Up

This is a story about a man named Robert Ebeling. He acted heroically. Mr. Ebeling had the integrity necessary to express the facts, and the courage to do what was right. Even when it was really difficult.

First, I want to tell you a not-so-significant story. Because it's this not-so-significant story that gives me the perspective to better appreciate Ebeling's heroism.

The CEO made a fist and slammed it on the conference room table. His face was red. Then he yelled, "Damn it, Triumph! Don't bring that up again."

A few weeks later I was fired. At the time, I was working for a medical device company that dominated the industry with more than a 70 percent global market share, and I was explaining (again) the product development roadmap. Specifically, the necessity of completing the development of the next generation product. It was a leapfrog product, and the frog we were hopping was ourselves.

We were having difficulties with the development (new materials weren't passing life-cycle testing), and it was during such a setback when I was making the case to carry on. Meanwhile, the CFO and his accountants were advocating killing the effort. One of them said (and I swear this is true), "The company hasn't had a new product for ten years, and we're doing just fine—so we don't even need a new product." So, I was let go just a few weeks after that occurred.

It was decades ago. It still kind of hurts, if you want to know the truth. Some years after my departure—having still not launched a new product—the company was reorganized and eventually completed the product development effort described previously. In fact, the same head of research and development (R&D) who originally patented the design, and was in the conference room for my chastising, was still there. His leapfrog design still dominates the industry and generates a few hundred million dollars annually.

Here's what you already know, despite the huge market share the company had, the world has a way of changing, and competitors have a way of competing. Progress isn't a direct unimpeded swagger into the future. So, it's obvious that a company needs to continually be improving its products.

But, at the time, evidently some people wanted to do what in the short-term must have seemed easier. No heroism on my part. Just a conviction to advocate professionally what I believed was best for the company. I stood up. I got fired. That's the not-so-significant story.

Now meet Robert Ebeling. Mr. Ebeling is a hero. Though like a lot of heroes, he certainly did not think of himself as such. In fact, for much of his life he thought he was a loser. He said so. Robert Ebeling was born in 1926. Maybe because his dad was a car mechanic, Ebeling had an affinity for mechanical things, and after several years as an infantryman in World War II, he got a degree in mechanical engineering from California Polytechnic State University in 1952.

After graduation, Ebeling moved to San Diego and worked for an aerospace company called Convair that made the first Atlas rockets used in Project Mercury—the first US human spaceflight program. He then joined a company called Thiokol in 1962 and eventually became the manager of ignition systems for the solid rocket boosters used for the Space Shuttle.

On January 27, 1986, 26 years after joining the company, which by then was called Morton Thiokol, Ebeling gathered data, and along with several other engineers argued passionately with their managers and with NASA management that the *Challenger* shuttle launch scheduled for the following day needed to be canceled.

The problem, they believed, was that the atypical cold temperatures that were then occurring in Florida would prevent the O-rings from properly sealing the rocket booster joints. They argued for hours that because of these conditions, a potential catastrophe was possible. But politics and pressures resulted in them being overruled by their managers and by NASA, and the lift-off was allowed to continue as planned, despite the cold overnight temperature of 18 degrees.

That next morning on January 28, Ebeling drove to work to watch the Shuttle launch from a large projector television screen. He took his daughter to work with him that day. He was sick with fear, and during the drive told his daughter, "The *Challenger* is going to blow up. Everyone's going to die." His daughter, Serna, recalled, "He was beating his fist on the dashboard. He was frantic."

Watching the launch, shortly after what appeared to be a successful liftoff, a fellow engineer told Ebeling, "We've just dodged a bullet." But, that was not the case. Just a minute later, the O-rings failed, and the *Challenger* erupted in flames and exploded. All seven crew members were killed.

Ebeling broke down and began sobbing. In some ways, he never recovered from the tragedy. "I've been under terrible stress since the accident. I have headaches. I cry. I have bad dreams. I go into a hypnotic trance almost daily." He left Morton Thiokol. He quit engineering. For decades he suffered with guilt.

On the thirtieth anniversary of the event, in January 2016, Ebeling told an NPR interviewer that, "I think this was one of the mistakes God made. He shouldn't have picked me for that job. I don't know, but next time I talk to him, I'm going to ask him 'Why? You picked a loser.'"

Hundreds of people who heard the broadcast wrote him letters of encouragement and understanding. Ebeling's old manager at Thiokol called to tell him that, "He was not a loser, that a loser was someone who has a chance to act but doesn't, and worse, doesn't care." The manager went on to explain that, Robert "really did do something." "If he had not called me, we never would have had the opportunity to try to avert the disaster. They would have just gone ahead with the launch. At least we had the opportunity to try to stop it."

Work is usually not a matter of life or death. In fact, for most of us what's at stake doesn't even compare to flying a rocket into space. But that's not an excuse for abdicating your voice, for not doing your best or sharing what you know, for looking the other way and "hoping for the best."

It often takes courage to speak up. And it's often important. As it turned out, Ebeling said all those letters of encouragement following his NPR interview greatly helped relieve his pain. "You helped bring my worrisome mind to ease," he said. "You have to have an end to everything."

Just a few months after his 30-year anniversary interview on NPR, after receiving all those letters, Robert Ebeling died. One of the listeners to that NPR broadcast was an engineer named Jim Sides. Sides said, "Bob Ebeling did his job. He did the right thing, and that does not make him a loser. That makes him a winner."

Monkeys Don't Build Rockets

In 2016, there was a loose gorilla onboard the *International Space Station* that chased the astronauts. Turns out it was astronaut Scott Kelly in a gorilla costume, pulling a prank on his colleagues. Although there have been chimpanzees in space … research shows they won't be building rockets, or sneaking onboard, anytime soon.

Andrew Whiten helped me understand this, and he knows a thing or two about chimpanzees and humans. He's an emeritus professor at the University of St. Andrews in the United Kingdom. He does fascinating research on the social behavior of nonhuman primates. Interesting work, especially because scientists have traditionally considered the chimp to be human's closest living relative—with a genetic difference of about 1.2 percent

In one of his groundbreaking research projects, Whiten and his researchers went to South Africa and studied 109 monkeys in the wild. The monkeys were in four different groups, and his team of researchers gave each group two trays filled with corn. In one of the trays, the corn was dyed blue, and in the other tray, the corn was dyed pink.

For two of the groups, the blue corn was made to taste bitter, and for the other two groups the pink corn was made to taste bitter. In each case, the respective corn was soaked in bitter aloe leaves. Within a short period of time, the monkeys all learned to completely ignore the bitter-tasting corn.

Four months later, after 27 little baby monkeys were born, the monkeys were again given the blue corn and the pink corn—although this time none of the corn was bitter. The adult monkeys all still avoided the color that previously tasted bitter. Even more surprising, the infant monkeys only ate the same corn as their mothers, although they had never even tasted or even actually knew there was such a thing as bitter corn.

Furthermore, during the time that the researchers were conducting the study, 10 adult male monkeys migrated from one of the groups to a different group that preferred the other color of corn. And 70 percent of those adult males quickly adopted the behavior of their new group and switched to eating the new preferred color.

Fortunately, at least some humans are more independent thinkers, and remain unswayed by social influences. Yvonne Brill was one such person. Brill was born in Canada in 1923 and, perhaps because her parents didn't graduate from high school, Yvonne recalled, "Education wasn't high on the agenda."

Brill enjoyed learning and did well in high school. Despite her acumen, she said, "None of the teachers particularly encouraged me. We had a male teacher for physics who just felt that women would never get anywhere."

Even the minor encouragement she received was misguided. The high school principal wanted her to go to a one-year preparatory teaching school after high school and get her teaching certificate so she could teach. She laughed when she remembered the advice, "And that just didn't sit well with me. I just felt I had more enterprise than that."

So she went to the University of Manitoba. At that time the university didn't allow women into its engineering program, so she graduated in math and chemistry at the top of her class at the age of 20. After graduation, she left for California and went to work for Douglas Aircraft on the design of the first US satellite. She simultaneously went to the University of Southern California in the evenings and got her master's degree in chemistry. Yvonne Brill was one of the first women working in rocket science!

She worked tirelessly, despite the challenging jobs and occasional criticism. When Brill got home at night, she fed her children and put them to bed. And then she would burn the midnight oil on an idea she had for a new type of rocket engine.

After years of after-hours work, calculating with a slide rule over the kitchen table in the wee hours of the night, Brill invented something called the hydrazine resistojet rocket engine. The rocket engine was more fuel efficient and offered increased performance. She patented the design in 1974.

Her engine concept was adopted first by one company and then another and eventually became a standard within the rocket industry. Brill's work contributed to the first weather satellite and rocket designs that were used on Moon missions. She received numerous awards in her lifetime, including the National Medal of Technology and Innovation presented to her by President Barack Obama.

Despite Yvonne Brill's incredible efforts and accomplishments, she always remained humble. "It wasn't that I was so great, I was just in the right place at the right time, which was really my good fortune." Actually, it seems more accurate that Yvonne Brill was in the wrong place at the wrong time, but didn't let those circumstances sway her.

Our genetics might be 98.8 percent identical to a chimpanzee, but the good news is that somewhere in the remaining, unique 1.2 percent, each of us is like Yvonne Brill. And that's all we need to build a rocket.

So, let's remember to try the different colored corn. Innovator Yvonne Brill would approve, and so would astronaut Scott Kelly in his gorilla suit.

Karma, and Why My Ex-Boss Might Go to Jail

I've always loved the song "Instant Karma" by John Lennon: "Instant Karma's gonna get you / Gonna look you right in the face / Better get yourself together darlin' / Join the human race."

Karma is the concept of "what goes around, comes around." It's the principle of cause and effect where intent and actions of an individual (cause) influence the future of that individual (effect). Good intent and good deed contribute to good karma and future happiness, while bad intent and bad deed contribute to bad karma and future suffering.

Sometimes, it's difficult to tell from just a couple of conversations with someone if they're a good person or a bad person. That's true, in part, because the bad person is doing his or her best to conceal their true identity and schemes from you.

It's also true because you perceive things through your own lens, which has been altered by your own predispositions, outlooks, and biases. So, whenever there are two people communicating with each other under these conditions, there's inherent margin for inaccuracy. Generally, my preset perspective is assuming people are genuine, hardworking, and have fair intentions. You're probably the same way.

At one point in my career, I was hired by the CEO of a small company. During the interview process, it was explained to me that the company was pioneering a breakthrough technology. It was building prototypes and planning more lab tests. However, after being hired, I was told to have zero involvement in that effort, because it wouldn't be commercialized until "some point in the future." Instead, I was directed to lead marketing and sales for the one other product that had been slow to gain traction.

I'm going to be purposefully vague here, but over the next few months, suffice it to say, I saw quite a bit of mismanagement and underperformance at the top level of the company. After several months I left. Hindsight has put the experience in the category of a consulting gig with bad management. The company isn't listed in my résumé or in my LinkedIn profile. I'd nearly forgotten about my time there.

Then, years after leaving the company, I tried visiting its website. Zilch! I then searched for the company online, and found articles describing how it had been closed, and the CEO had been convicted of tax evasion and was still on trial for allegedly defrauding investors. I was shocked. But not wholly surprised.

I was not entirely surprised because of issues that became increasingly apparent during my time there. And there's no shortage of other business, societal, and political leadership misdeeds—Bernie Madoff's Ponzi scheme, Volkswagen's emissions scandal, the Fédération Internationale de Football Association (FIFA) racketeering, fake Wells Fargo accounts—to remind us that greedy behavior is not rare.

My predisposition still remains that people are generally well-intentioned and have the goodwill of others in mind. But, I realize that's not always the case. I like the idea of karma, of good people coming out on top. But, I realize that's not always the case.

It seems obvious that the goal every day should be to get wiser and better. Live and love more. Start with yourself, and spread it out to your family, friends, colleagues, and clients. We're humans, and our history, albeit with an objectionable number of setbacks, is to advance toward improvement. So, onward we go trying to do the right thing. Hopefully making even a small contribution in the right direction.

I think that's what John Lennon meant. "Well we all shine on / Like the moon and the stars and the sun / Well we all shine on / Ev'ryone come on."

After reading about that conniving CEO being on trial, I found the name of the detective investigating the case and called him the next day to inquire if I could be of any help.

Your First Exam and the Butterfly Effect

I like the idea that everything matters. That each of us—through the work we do, through even our seemingly inconsequential interactions—has an impact on others. And furthermore, that it's not just the work we do, but that our efforts and intentions matter too. That might seem like a soft argument, but it's actually an easy one to validate for ourselves.

Think about it, we've certainly all been inspired and affected by people who fought tirelessly and valiantly, whether it was for a just cause or against an illness, even if they lost the battle in the end. History is full of such examples that inspire and motivate. And given the construct that what we do affects others, it follows that the results from what we do either fall on the contributing side or the negative side of this "impact ledger."

Here's something else that's important to understand. It's often difficult to predict just how much good might come from our efforts. What we might regard as a seemingly minor suggestion—might provide that first critical spark necessary to ignite a new way of thinking. Or our lending a hand might just be one more drop in a necessary change toward a fundamental societal shift. But in either scenario—it matters.

The concept that small causes can have large effects is often described as the "butterfly effect." The concept originated in the early 1800s, and was advanced by Ray Bradbury in his fictional writing and by Edward Lorenz within the science of meteorology. The term was coined by American scientist and meteorologist Lorenz to describe how seemingly small things can have a huge impact.

This was evidenced mathematically when Lorenz was using a computer model to determine weather predictions. When he entered an initial condition of 0.506 rather than the precise value of 0.506127—the resulting weather prediction model was astoundingly different.

(Of course, it's also difficult to predict how much harm can come if our contributions are on the negative side of the ledger, but let's focus on the positive.)

Here's one story about how a seemingly simple and small idea actually had big consequences—and … it involved you. Chances are you don't even know this story, but it's true. It begins with the person who was responsible for your first exam (actually, your first two exams). And then how your exam results were then used as another drop in an ocean of data to bring clarity to previously unseen and unknown insights, which have since been credited with saving the lives of tens of thousands of babies every year in the US

Allow me to introduce you to the person responsible for your first exams. Her name is Virginia Apgar. She was a woman of integrity and persistence, of intelligence and character. She had your best health in mind. And Virginia Apgar always strove to make contributions on the positive side of the ledger.

Apgar was born in 1909. The world was a different place. Henry Ford had just introduced the Model T, the Morse code distress signal or SOS (three dots, three dashes, three dots) had recently became the worldwide standard, and the first boxes of Crayola Crayons were just a few years old. There was also significant sexism and racial inequities. Fortunately for you, Virginia Apgar didn't let the sexism and inequities of the day slow her down.

Apgar was an active child, did well in school, and loved music. Perhaps because her father died from tuberculosis, and because her brother had health issues, Apgar decided to become a doctor.

She went to Columbia University College of Physicians and Surgeons in 1933. Due to the fact that no university would provide her with a scholarship or financial aid because she was a woman, Apgar graduated with substantial debt, even though she was fourth in her class.

After graduation, her advisor explained to her that it'd be difficult for her to succeed as a surgeon because there were basically no other female surgeons, and patients would be unlikely to choose her. So, he encouraged her to study the newly emerging field of anesthesiology, explaining that she had the "energy, intelligence, and ability needed to make significant contributions in this area." It was a difficult decision, but Apgar thought the idea made sense.

After completing the six-month anesthesiology program at the University of Wisconsin-Madison, Apgar spent another six months in the anesthesiology program at Bellevue Hospital in New York, before returning to Columbia University as the director of the division of anesthesia.

During her work at Columbia University College of Physicians and Surgeons, Apgar observed there was no adequate means of assessing the overall health of newborn babies. There were, of course, some obvious indications, such as if the baby was breathing or pink, but there was not a standardized means of consistently scoring the baby's health.

Apgar decided a simple, yet comprehensive system was needed, and she came up with a rating system to quickly assess the health of newborn babies. The system involved five parameters: skin color, heart rate, reflex irritability, muscle tone, and respiration. Each characteristic was then scored 0, 1, or 2.

Perhaps, not surprisingly, the idea was met with resistance, yet it was grudgingly put into practice where she worked. The aggregate score, which could range from 0 to 10, was both simple and effective. The exam and scoring were done at one minute and five minutes after the baby was born. The rating system and the one-minute and five-minute examinations spread to other hospitals throughout the US.

A few years later, an intern using the methodology at a hospital in Denver, Colorado, came up with an acronym for the practice that used her name Apgar: appearance (skin color), pulse (heart rate), grimace (reflex irritability), activity (muscle tone), and respiration. The scoring became ubiquitous in hospitals throughout the United States and around the world.

As physician Atul Gawande wrote in *The New Yorker,*

"The score was published in 1953, and it transformed child delivery. It turned an intangible and impressionistic clinical concept—the condition of a newly born baby—into a number that people could collect and compare. Using it required observation and documentation of the true condition of every baby. Moreover, even if only because doctors are competitive, it drove them to want to produce better scores—and therefore better outcomes—for the newborns they delivered."[56]

What's more, when the two scores for one minute and five minutes were aggregated into hundreds of thousands of other numbers—physicians and healthcare analysts were able to clearly discern trends that previously had been hidden. The numbers gave meaningful insight into the health of the baby, and if the baby was in danger. You were one of those babies.

The data showed physicians with statistical significance how the health of babies varied, depending on what anesthetics were used or not used. This led to significant insights and changes in neonatal practices.

As Dr. Gawande wrote, "If the statistics of 1940 had persisted, fifteen thousand mothers would have died last year (instead of fewer than five hundred)—and a hundred and twenty thousand newborns (instead of one-sixth that number)."[57]

Virginia Apgar was both honest and tenacious in her quest to improve healthcare, and she was without ego. She always made it a habit to carry a pocketknife and tubing in her purse, in case someone needed an emergency tracheotomy. She said nobody was going to suffocate in her presence.

Once, after one of her patients died following surgery, Virginia feared that perhaps she had mistakenly clamped a vessel during the surgery that could have contributed to the patient's demise. Although Virginia didn't have permission, she snuck into the morgue, reopened the closed incision and saw that she had in fact ligated the vessel in question. Virginia immediately reported what she discovered to the chief of staff. Learning was of paramount importance to her, and she steadfastly pursued improved patient outcomes.

Years later, after she worked tirelessly building the anesthesiology division, it was decided that it would become a stand-alone department. The director of that new department was given to a man. But Apgar took what must have certainly seemed like a slight in stride and continued forward. She then got her master's degree in public health from Johns Hopkins University in 1959.

She published over 60 journal articles, wrote a popular book with Joan Beck titled *Is My Baby All Right?* and assisted in delivering nearly 20,000 babies. So, thanks to Virginia Apgar for creating the Apgar score. And thank you for taking the exam (twice) and contributing the data that continues to help save tens of thousands of lives a year.

Turns out, seemingly small things can have a huge impact. Just ask any baby.

How to Crush Your Fears, Innovate, and Hug a Snake

Say what?! Turns out, ophidiophobia is one of the most common fears people have. It's a fear held by Justin Timberlake, Matt Damon, and even Indiana Jones. In fact, it's a fear held by an estimated 30 percent of the population!

Ophidiophobia is the abnormal fear of snakes. And ophidiophobes aren't just fearful when they're in the presence of snakes—they're mostly terrified even when just thinking about them. And, of course, it's not just snakes that large percentages of people fear. A similarly large percentage of people fear heights, or public speaking, or even change itself. There are fears holding you back from doing your best creative and entrepreneurial work.

Brothers David and Tom Kelley can tell you a lot about those fears holding you back from your creative confidence. They have decades of real-world experience building their creative confidence and helping thousands of others do the same.

David Kelley is the founder of the design firm IDEO, founder of Stanford University's Hasso Plattner Institute of Design, and has taught design classes for nearly four decades. His brother, Tom Kelley, is a partner at IDEO and teaches at Berkeley. Together the Kelley brothers have written several books on creativity and innovation.

IDEO has done work for some of the world's most highly regarded brands, and their work has led the way for thousands of innovations, many of them revolutionary and across a wide variety of industries. IDEO designed the first useable computer mouse, groundbreaking nonprofit programs, and digital tools to help people with schizophrenia. The Kelley brothers, and their several hundred colleagues at IDEO, know about the fears inherent in creativity.

Here are four fears they've identified that all too often hold people back from their creative confidence.

1. Fear of the Messy Unknown

   It's an understatement to describe venturing into new territory as uncomfortable. The truth is that venturing down a new path is stressful—whether developing a new product, exploring a new line of business, or pursuing a new career. The unknown is messy and often painful.

   Gone is the certainty (real or imagined) of "business as usual." When you're in pursuit of something new, whatever thrill existed of the unknown fades and you're left with uncertainty, stumbling down dead ends and making mistakes.

2. Fear of Being Judged

   This is something we've feared since we were kids—being judged. We're afraid of not knowing the answer, failing or fumbling—and looking foolish as a result. We've taken those experiences of criticism and internalized them to the extent that we can imagine the criticism before we've even made an attempt. And the fear stops us.

3. Fear of the First Step

   It's easy to delay getting started. For one thing, things aren't fully planned out. What's more, it's easy to come up with a bunch of reasons as to why today is not the right day to get started.

4. Fear of Losing Control

   When we apply our creativity to a new venture—when we take a creative leap, or try something new—things get messy. The new work feels disordered. The new process seems haphazard. By comparison, what we used to do seemed well-ordered and provided the feeling of something we could control. The customer, offering, and means of measuring success were understood. But when we're creating something new, the instability is palpable.

So, the question becomes, how do we overcome those fears that are inhibiting or arresting our creative confidence?

Well, that brings us back to ophidiophobia and Professor Al Bandura of Stanford University. Professor Bandura is regarded as one of the greatest figures in psychology for his work related to social cognitive theory and self-efficacy. He's a frequently cited psychologist and one of the most influential psychologists of all time. And he is able to take people who were completely terrified at the thought of a snake and help them become comfortable handling a live one within just hours.

One of the therapy factors in helping people overcome their fear of snakes was by simply having them observe other people with ophidiophobia who had become comfortable handling snakes. The patients in treatment internalized the information that if others like them handled snakes with no ill effects, then they could do the same. Bandura found that these observations were more effective in treating the phobias than persuasion and observing the psychologist handle the snakes.

In addition, Bandura also had his patients imitate and model this behavior. More important, Professor Bandura has shown how the same techniques of observing others, imitating, and modeling can be used to overcome essentially any fear. Even those fears holding you back from doing your best creative and entrepreneurial work.

So, how does the work of this preeminent psychologist apply to building your creative confidence? We can start by recognizing what fear might be holding us back from applying our creativity—whether it's the fear of the unknown, being judged, taking that first step, or losing control. And then we observe others who overcame those same fears, imitating their behaviors and modeling their processes.

In fact, what we fear is likely indicating exactly what we should be working on overcoming. After all, the future is ahead—in those unchartered and unknown territories.

Nobody said it better than Tom and Dave Kelley of IDEO: "Don't get ready, get started!" Getting started is probably why vaudeville comedian W. C. Fields said, "I like to keep a bottle of stimulant handy in case I see a snake, which I also keep handy."

How to Die Broke and Not Broken

Here are two absolutely true stories of two different people. I know which one you'd want to be. While at one point, their stories are somewhat similar, their paths markedly diverge in dramatic contrast. One person finishes life as a multibillionaire. The other person has steered his life into a rapid economic decline. You want to be the one who experienced the rapid economic decline.

Adolph Merkel was born into a wealthy German family and proved to be a force of nature in the business world. He took over his family's already sizable chemical business and applied his business acumen to transforming it into the country's largest pharmaceutical wholesaler called Phoenix Pharmahandel. He didn't stop there.

He then founded Germany's first generic pharmaceutical company and later went on to invest in diverse businesses, including construction materials and manufacturing. In 2007, he was a successful businessman, a husband, a father of four grown children, and one of the wealthiest people in the world with what *Forbes Magazine* estimated at $12.8 billion.

In the following year, some poorly timed investments resulted in his wealth declining to about $9 billion. Although still one of the top 100 richest people in the entire world, the losses were devastating to Adolf Merkel. A couple of weeks after Christmas 2009, he committed suicide by throwing himself in front of a train near his home.

The other story is about Chuck Feeney. Chuck Feeney was an American college student at Cornell. With one of his classmates, and soon-to-be business partner, he came upon the idea of selling duty-free products to service personnel in Asia. They started selling liquor, but quickly added other items and eventually branched into including luxury products. If you've been in an airport, you've certainly seen (and probably been to) one of his duty-free stores.

Feeney was born during the Depression and has always been frugal and low-maintenance. Despite having a global business, Feeney flew economy class, never owned a car, and lived in a rented apartment. Going out to a restaurant for fine dining meant sitting at Tommy Makem's Irish Pavilion on East 57th Street in New York City and eating a hamburger.

He's married to a lovely wife, has five grown children, and oh, by the way, a net worth of $8 billion dollars. Well, actually, he *did* have a net worth of $8 billion. In 1982, he decided to give it all away. By 2016, Feeney accomplished exactly that. Chuck Feeney gave away his entire fortune and he did so anonymously.

Because of his secrecy and success and charm (I'm guessing at charm, because it's probably impossible to be that unbelievably kind and generous without being one of the most charming humans in world), Feeney has been called the "James Bond of philanthropy." *TIME* magazine said that, "Feeney's beneficence ranks among the grandest of any living American."[58]

Adolph Merkel was worth $9 billion dollars when he took his own life. Chuck Feeney was worth $8 billion when he decided to give it all away.

These events bring to mind Francis Bacon's comment that "Money is a great servant but a bad master." My guess is Chuck Feeney understands that too.

The Product Roadmap of You

Let's say you started here. A frail, chronically sick kid, with continuous coughs, frequent colds, bouts of fevers, diarrhea. Asthma so bad, at times your family fears it'll be fatal. Sometimes it feels like you're being suffocated with a pillow pushed over your face. Then, when you're about 12 years old, a doctor advises your parents that getting fresh air and exercise would be good for you, as physical conditioning will help strengthen your weak and damaged lungs.

So, your dad (or mom) tells you, "You have the mind but not the body, and without the help of the body the mind cannot go as far as it should. I am giving you the tools, but it is up to you to make your body." You're 12. What plans would you make? What course would you maintain?

A roadmap for business growth and product development is an essential part of today's world. It's basically a plan for how and when the short-term goals will be accomplished, how these align and fit with the longer-term objectives. Of course, it's not expected that completing a roadmap will result in an exact forecast of future events or an immutable blueprint, but it is, nonetheless, an important exercise in planning a successful way forward.

Where a business is concerned, the roadmap considers how the guiding strategies might evolve to meet anticipated market changes, or what business development efforts should be pursued to maintain competitiveness and grow. Where product development is concerned, the roadmap provides the plan as to how the offering will evolve, segment into new markets, and expand with line extensions. It represents the thinking toward future success and anticipates a changing environment—whether those changes are economic, political, competitive, technological, or social.

Simply, a roadmap is a plan to get from point A to point B. It's real-world stuff, so the roadmap should be regularly revisited and revised as necessary. A roadmap is what allowed Walmart to go from one store and several employees in 1962 to 11,718 stores and 2.3 million employees in 2017.

A roadmap is what grew Coca-Cola from serving its first drink in 1886 to a company with over 3,500 different beverages. As for the Coca-Cola drink—as the company notes in its history, "If all the Coca-Cola ever produced were in 8-ounce contour bottles, and these bottles were laid end to end, they would reach to the moon and back 2,051 times. That is one round trip per day for five years, seven months and 14 days."[59]

A roadmap is what Amazon founder Jeff Bezos and the leadership team use to guide the focus on better serving customers, expanding into new products, and increasing operational efficiencies. Amazon began in 1995 as an e-commerce company selling books. There was a bell in the office that would ring whenever an order came in. It was removed after just a few weeks because it was ringing continuously. In 2017, Amazon accounts for over 40 percent of all online sales, uses 45,000 robots across its fulfillment centers, and sells what seems like *everything*!

No company or product should be without a roadmap that considers the big picture, the growth strategy, the initiatives to meet market demands, the plans for product capabilities, and how to add greater value to its customers. But, what about you? What's your roadmap?

When the 12-year-old boy was told by his dad, "It is up to you to make your body," Theodore Roosevelt immediately responded, "I will make my body." And so young Teddy began a disciplined and consistent effort of engaging in strenuous, physical activity every day. He would exercise in the gym and go for long hikes in the mountains. He took up weight lifting and boxing. Similar to a business or product roadmap, Roosevelt took himself on a journey of growth and improvement. As with any roadmap, it was replete with revisions, setbacks, and difficulties.

While there aren't many organizations today that operate their business or product lines without a roadmap, my guess is the majority of people forgo having one for themselves. That's a mistake.

In the case of Theodore Roosevelt, he grew strong and went on to accomplish great things.

- Became the youngest US president to date, at age 42

- Was awarded (posthumously) a Congressional Medal of Honor

- Established national parks and created the US Forest Service

- Championed the Panama Canal

- Passed workmen's compensation laws

- Won the Nobel Peace Prize

Nobody would suggest a product roadmap guarantees success (or that your likeness will be carved onto Mount Rushmore), but it is a useful guide in charting your course.

Like Roosevelt said, "Do what you can, with what you have, where you are."

What Your Tomorrow Should Feel Like

He was hoping to be dead by Christmas. My heart sank when he told me this. We'd never met in person. He told me this over the phone about a year ago. I've been discouraged before, but couldn't imagine what he must have been feeling.

He had a successful business, but he explained personal disappointments in other areas of his life piled up, and at some point the tangle of setbacks turned into despair. And over time the unabated despair made a dive toward hopelessness. Everything grew heavy. He lost interest in moving forward. He lost interest in a tomorrow.

I listened and urged him to see a counselor and a doctor. Sometimes we need help to get back on track. Whatever help it takes … I'm all for that.

Occasionally inspiration works. It's a reminder of the promise and possibility in tomorrow, and in the days after tomorrow.

Bill Murray, comedian and Academy Award Best Actor nominee, tells the story of how a painting helped save his life, or at least got him thinking in the right direction. It was early in his career and after a first experience acting, he walked out of the theatre disappointed with his terrible performance.

"I was so bad that I just walked out afterward and onto the street. I kept walking for a couple of hours. Then I realized that I walked in the wrong direction and not in just the wrong direction from where I lived, but in the desire to stay alive.... I ended up in front of the Art

*Institute and walked inside. There was a painting of a woman working
in a field with a sunrise behind her. I always loved that painting."*[60]

The painting was done by the artist Jules Breton in 1884. It is of a young, peasant woman in a field. She's gazing into the distance, as she listens to the songbird. The sun is just starting to rise in the background, bringing a warm glow to the field and her face.

Bill explains what he saw in the painting. "Look, there's a girl without a lot of prospects, but the sun's coming up and she's got another chance at it.... I said 'I'm a person, too, and will get another chance every single day."

*"Don't think about your errors or failures;
otherwise, you'll never do a thing."*
—Bill Murray

Acknowledgments

A heartfelt thank you to the many wonderful people with whom I've worked over the years. You've inspired and informed my thinking as to what it means to do good work.

A special thank you to the folks and friends whose deep knowledge and patient explanations have made the book richer and me a better person: Mary Ann Badalli, Bill Briggs, Victor Cascella, Stephen Chakwin, Richard D'Aveni, Peter DiGasbarro, Esther Dyson, Anders Ericsson, Don Farrell, Robin Freedman, Linda Ginzel, Kartik Hosanagar, Earl Miller, Frank Musorrafiti, Graeme Newell, Carl Nordgren, Stan Phelps, Tom Salisbury, Robert Schock, Patrick Schruben, John Sculley, Marshall Ulrich, and Doug Vaughan. And, of course, to my mom and dad.

A sincere thank you to Joni Wilson for your editing prowess and to Kerry Ellis for your cover and interior creative design.

And I could not be more thankful for my family and for your support during my ultraruns (where admittedly CREW sometimes is an acronym for "Crabby Runner, Endless Waiting").

Thank You

A sincere thank you for reading my book. If you enjoyed it, please pass it along and kindly take a minute to leave me a review.

Subscribe

Learn how to better innovate—and transform your work, business and life. www.tomtriumph.com

Let's Start a Conversation

For general inquires or to say hello, reach me at tom@tomtriumph.com.

About the Author

Thomas Triumph helps companies grow by collaboratively helping them reinvent their business, product development, and marketing. Along the way he's helped large organizations act nimbly and small companies scale.

He's been a participant in two technology revolutions—less invasive surgery and software—and has been part of some remarkable success stories (and some misfires).

He fulfilled a childhood dream of living aboard an ocean research ship and tending to the mini-sub (Cousteau was on the Board), wrestled in the Olympic trials, and helped oversee the design and fabrication of the largest composite hovercraft ever built in the US. He resides in North Carolina and is an ultrarunner who envies Tom Hanks' long run as Forrest Gump.

Notes

This Is Your Secret Superpower

1. Thanks to Ed Brubaker, author of *Batman*.

Ten Ways to Rewire Your Brain

2. "Temporal and Spatial Dynamics of Brain Structure Changes during Extensive Learning." *Journal of Neuroscience*. June 7, 2006. https://www.ncbi.nlm.nih.gov/pubmed/16763039

3. "Eight Weeks to a Better Brain." *The Harvard Gazette*. January 21, 2011. https://news.harvard.edu/gazette/story/2011/01/eight-weeks-to-a-better-brain/

4. "How Much Do We Love TV? Let Us Count the Ways." *The New York Times*. June 30, 2016. https://www.nytimes.com/2016/07/01/business/media/nielsen-survey-media-viewing.html

5. See *Alive Inside* trailer at https://www.imdb.com/title/tt2593392/videoplayer/vi2662247449?ref_=tt_ov_vi

Thoughts on Life and Happiness

6. Bob Fronterhouse. *The Liberal Leanings of the Liberating Lamb*. Lulu Publishing. 2016.

Rules for Creating Your Future (from a Rock Guitarist)

7. "Soft Skills, Hard Questions." Drucker Institute. November 11, 2013. http://www.druckerinstitute.com/2013/11/soft-skills-hard-questions/

8. Steve Vai interviewed by Justin Sandercoe. February 25, 2013. http://how-do-you-play-guitar.com/?p=513

Love Over Gold

9. "For the Love of Money." *The New York Times*. January 18, 2014. https://www.nytimes.com/2014/01/19/opinion/sunday/for-the-love-of-money.html

One, Two, Three, Four (Drum Intro)
10. "Art" https://en.wikipedia.org/wiki/Art

The Multitasking Myth
11. "Think You're Multitasking? Think Again." NPR. October 2, 2008. https://www.npr.org/templates/story/story.php?storyId=95256794

12. "Nov. 10, 1999: Metric Math Mistake Muffed Mars Meteorology Mission." *Wired*. November 10, 2010. https://www.wired.com/2010/11/1110mars-climate-observer-report/

Lessons to Teach Your Children
13. "How Many Stars, Planets and Black Holes Are in Our Galaxy?" *Explorist*. March 4, 2017. https://explorist.futurism.com/how-many-stars-planets-and-black-holes-are-in-the-milky-way-galaxy/

14. "There Are 37.2 Trillion Cells in Your Body." Smithsonian. Com. October 24, 2013.

What Running (Far) Has Taught Me about Work and Life

15. "Marshall Ulrich." https://en.wikipedia.org/wiki/Marshall_Ulrich

16. "David Goggins." https://en.wikipedia.org/wiki/David_Goggins

Think Like an Immigrant
17. "The Immigrant Advantage." *The New York Times*. May 24, 2014. https://www.nytimes.com/2014/05/25/opinion/sunday/the-immigrant-advantage.html

18. "The 'New American' Fortune 500." June 2011. https://www.newamericaneconomy.org/sites/all/themes/pnae/img/new-american-fortune-500-june-2011.pdf

A Billion Hours of Accidental Love
19. "What Did Einstein Mean By 'You Can't Blame Gravity for Falling in Love'?" Quora. October 23, 2016. https://www.quora.com/What-did-Einstein-mean-by-You-cant-blame-gravity-for-falling-in-love

Disastrous Problem + Resounding Failure = World-Changing Success
20. *The Evening Independent*. February 22, 1934. https://www.newspapers.com/newspage/4250853/

21. Eddie Rickenbacker. *Seven Came Through*. Doubleday, 1943.

Advice for Your Journey
22. Joseph Campbell. *The Hero with a Thousand Faces*. New World Library. 2008, p. 23.

23. Steve Jobs—The Lost Interview. https://www.youtube.com/watch?v=tBh5_j4a1yo

Twenty of the Greatest Inventions of All Time

24. "Steve Jobs on Why Computers Are Like a Bicycle for the Mind (1990)." https://www.brainpickings.org/2011/12/21/steve-jobs-bicycle-for-the-mind-1990/

25. "What's the Greatest Invention of All Time?" *The Economist*. January/February 2012. https://www.1843magazine.com/intelligence/the-big-question/whats-the-greatest-invention-of-all-time

26. "The 50 Greatest Breakthroughs Since the Wheel." The Atlantic. November 2013. https://www.theatlantic.com/magazine/archive/2013/11/innovations-list/309536/

Moving the Bullseye

27. "Steve Jobs on Simple Design." June 8, 2016. https://plus.google.com/+Geeksdemycom/posts/NyPkf4UHHUE

Turnaround Test

28. Peter Drucker. *Innovation and Entrepreneurship*. Routledge. 2015, p. 280.

29. "Apple's Top 10 Tips for Great Product Design." *Computerworld*. January 7, 2015. https://www.computerworld.com/article/2866054/apples-top-10-tips-for-great-product-design.html

The Woman Whose Magic Is Five Times Stronger Than Steel
30. "'You've Got to Find What You Love,' Jobs Says." *Stanford News*. June 14, 2005. https://news.stanford.edu/2005/06/14/jobs-061505/

31. "Inspiring Inventor: Stephanie Kwolek (1923–2014)." *Lemelson Center*. June 24, 2014. http://invention.si.edu/inspiring-inventor-stephanie-kwolek-1923-2014

Ladies and Gentlemen, the Greatest of All Inventors Is ...
32. "Stanley D. Stookey." National Medal of Technology and Innovation. https://www.nationalmedals.org/laureates/stanley-d-stookey

From Humble Beginnings: Secrets of World-Class Innovators and Creators
33. *The Reader's Digest*. September 1947, p. 64.

34. "The Role of Deliberate Practice in the Acquisition of Expert Performance." *Psychological Review*. 1993.

Garbage In, a Billion Dollars Out

35. "The Top 11 Doritos Commercials of All Time." https://www.youtube.com/watch?v=dWdfUBajb4I

Find What You Love and Let It Kill You

36. "James Rhodes: 'Find What You Love and Let It Kill You.'" *The Guardian*. April 26, 2013. https://www.theguardian.com/music/musicblog/2013/apr/26/james-rhodes-blog-find-what-you-love

37. "JRhodesPianist." https://soundcloud.com/jrhodespianist

Counterintuitive Secrets to Grow Your Career
38. "Why I Love Haters." *Medium*. November 12, 2014. https://medium.com/@brentonhayden/why-i-love-haters-f6b12fae47d4

39. "Why You Should Listen." https://www.ted.com/speakers/william_ury

The Secret to Great Work

40. "Penn Jillette: The Brilliant Idea Can Kill You." https://jamesaltucher.com/2015/09/penn-jillette-the-brilliant-idea-can-kill-you/

Survival Lessons from the First Fish in Space

41. "47% of Jobs will Disappear in the Next 25 Years, According to Oxford University." *Big Think*. https://bigthink.com/philip-perry/47-of-jobs-in-the-next-25-years-will-disappear-according-to-oxford-university

A Hypercompetitive World: Globalization and Technology
42. "Energy Drinks Market Analysis By Product." July 2017. https://www.grandviewresearch.com/industry-analysis/energy-drinks-market

43. Professor Richard D'Aveni is from the Tuck School of Business at Dartmouth, winner of the prestigious A. T. Kearney Award for research and a recognized leading worldwide strategy consultant. D'Aveni is often ranked in the top 20 management thinkers and a top five strategist by the Thinkers50.

What It Feels Like to Punch Fear in the Face
44. Check out his artwork at this website: http://www.artnet.com/artists/chuck-close/

45. "Agnes," Sartle Rogue Art Gallery. https://www.sartle.com/artwork/agnes-chuck-close

46. Toby Karten, *Building on the Strengths of Students with Special Needs: How to Move Beyond Disability Labels in the Classroom*. ACSD. 2017. p. 116.

47. "Chuck Close at His Gala Party: Eff You Every Much," September 21, 2007. http://www.vulture.com/2007/09/chuck_close_at_his_gala_party. html

48. Adapted from an unsourced quote attributed to George Bernard Shaw.

A Proven Technique for Producing Ideas

49. Barry Miles. *The Beatles Diary Volume 1: The Beatle Years*. Omnibus Press, 2009.

50. Miles. *The Beatles Diary Volume 1*.

51. "The Paul McCartney Encyclopedia." http://www.wingspan.ru/book-seng/encyclopedia/y.html

52. "Paul McCartney's 'Scrambled Eggs,' Which Evolved into One of the Most Recorded Songs of All Time." *Today I Found Out*. October 15, 2014. http://www.todayifoundout.com/index.php/2014/10/paul-mccartneys-yesterday/

Becoming a Creative Genius (Again)

53. Carl Nordgren. *Becoming a Creative Genius {Again}*. Torchflame Books. 2016.

The Twelve Dimensions of Courage

54. Tom Moon. *1,000 Recordings to Hear Before You Die*. Workman Publishing Company. 2008. P. 208.

55. "Ballet Dancer Leaps onto Subway Tracks and Lifts Man to Safety." *The New York Times*. June 4, 2017. https://www.nytimes. com/2017/06/04/arts/dance/ballet-dancer-gray-davis-subway-rescue. html

Your First Exam and the Butterfly Effect

56. "The Score." *The New Yorker*. October 9, 2006. https://www.newy-orker.com/magazine/2006/10/09/the-score

57. "The Score."

How to Die Broke and Not Broken

58. "Others Who Shaped 1997: Charles Feeney." *TIME*. December 29, 1997.

The Product Roadmap of You

59. "125 Years of Sharing Happiness: A Short History of The Coca-Cola Company." https://www.coca-colacompany.com/content/dam/journey/us/en/private/fileassets/pdf/2011/05/Coca-Cola_125_years_booklet.pdf

What Your Tomorrow Should Feel Like
60. "The Art Institute Moment That Saved Bill Murray's Career." *Chicago Sun-Times.* July 24, 2018. https://chicago.suntimes.com/entertainment/the-art-institute-moment-that-saved-bill-murrays-career/

35431268R00150

Made in the USA
Middletown, DE
05 February 2019